GET DOWN!!

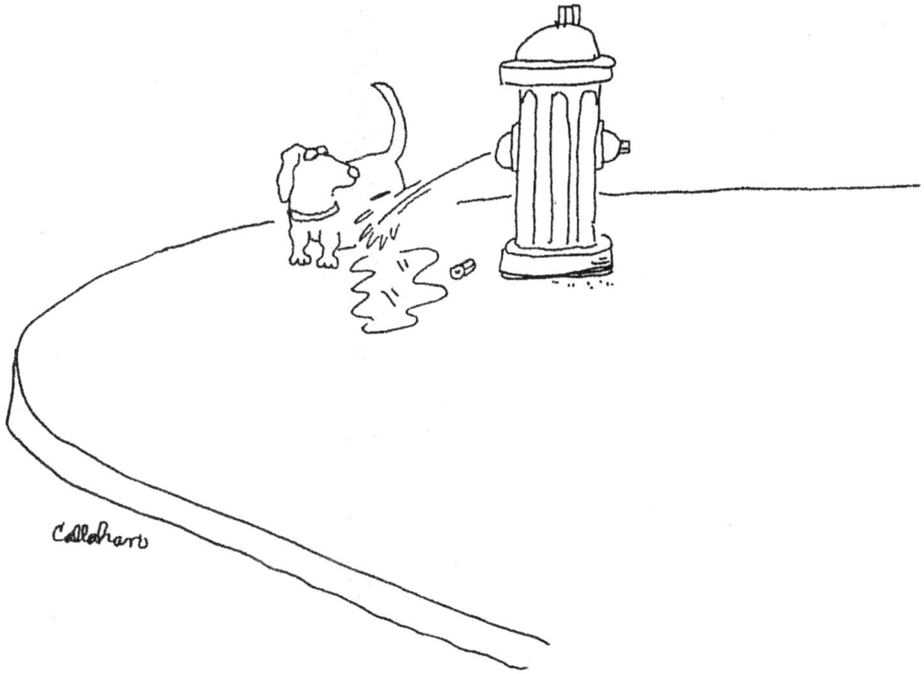
Callahan

Dog Cartoons by Callahan

Ballantine Books • New York

A Ballantine Book
Published by The Ballantine Publishing Group

Copyright © 2002 by John Callahan ·

All rights reserved under International and Pan-American Copyright Conventions. Published in the United States by The Ballantine Publishing Group, a division of Random House, Inc., New York, and simultaneously in Canada by Random House of Canada Limited, Toronto.

A portion of this work was originally published in syndicated form.

Ballantine and colophon are registered trademarks of Random House, Inc.

www.ballantinebooks.com

Library of Congress Catalog Card Number: 2002090181

ISBN 0-345-45093-0

Cover design by Carl Galian

Manufactured in the United States of America

First Edition: June 2002

10 9 8 7 6 5 4 3 2 1

GET DOWN!!

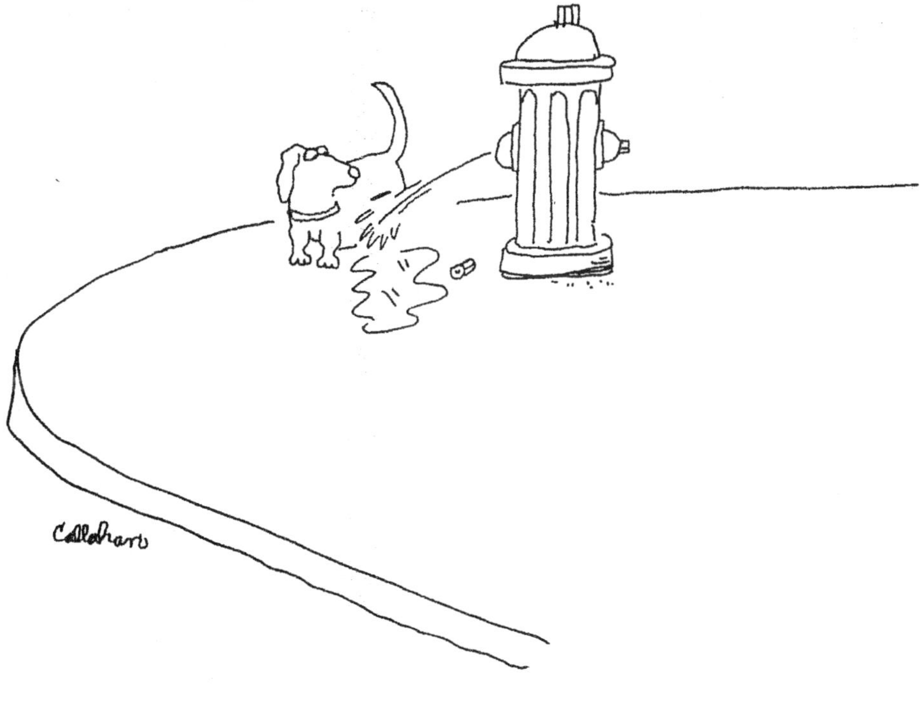
Callahan

'TOO WET FOR WEENIE!'

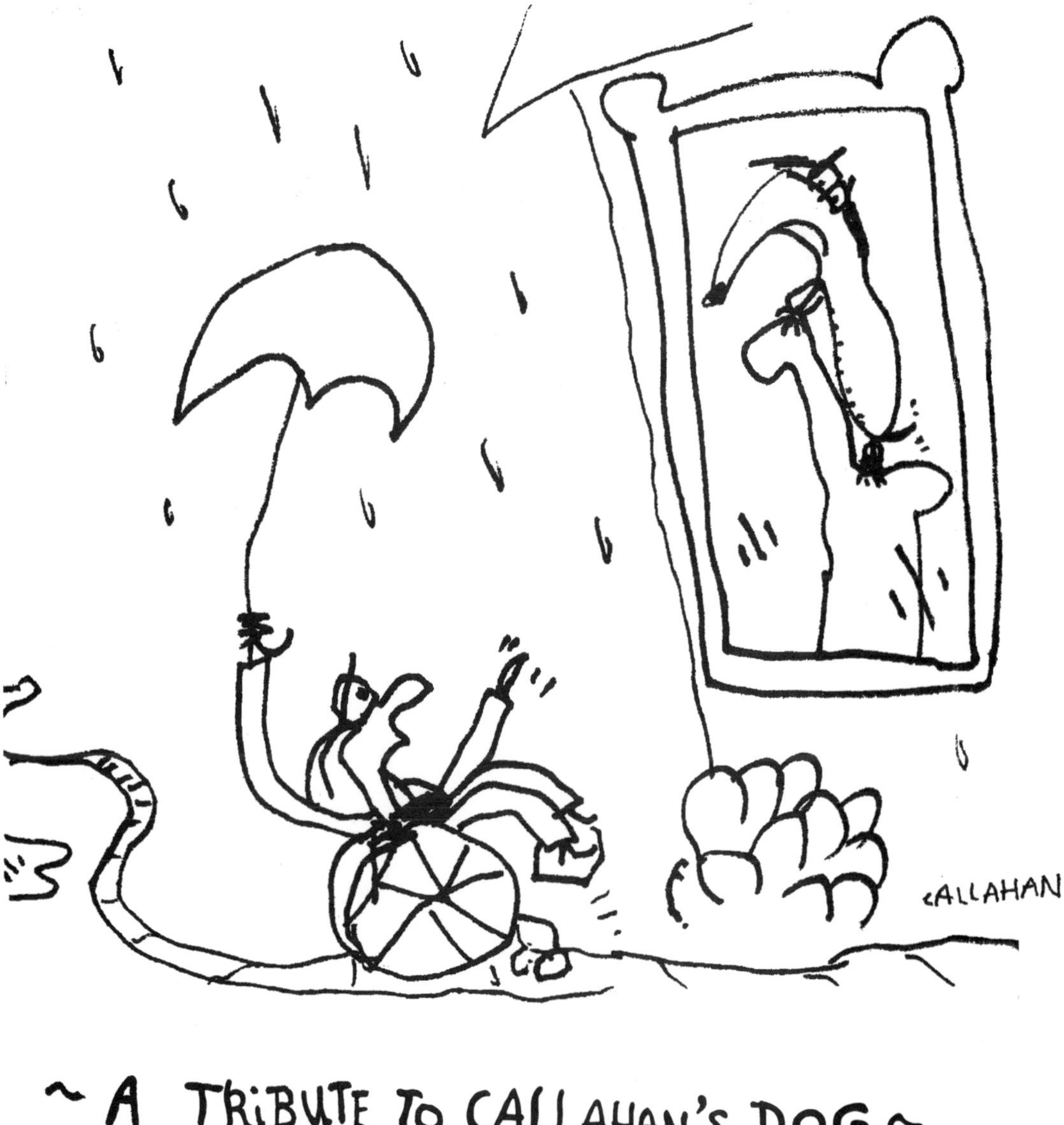
CALLAHAN

~ A TRIBUTE TO CALLAHAN'S DOG ~

There are some dogs that change your life. Weenie was such a dog. From the time she came to me at the age of nine till the day she passed at fourteen, she took control of the entire household—actually, the entire block! On summer nights she would walk through the neighbor's open front door and attempt to stridently "bark them" out of their own home! If you looked up the word "territorial" in the dictionary, you'd see Weenie's picture next to it! She was either severely delusional or totally lionhearted. Once, when she was sitting here with me on the front porch, Weenie attacked a giant Doberman ten times her size! Though the Doberman headed her backward right

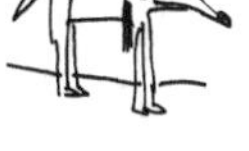

back up the wheelchair ramp, you could still hear the <u>ferocity</u> in the pitiful "half yelp–half bark" she courageously managed to blather out. She took great care of me, too. Like a little old lady she would jump up her little series of stools and pounce on the foot of my bed, bounding along the bedspread on her stumpy wiener dog legs, up to give me a light peck on the cheek, and then settling precisely in between my ankles. Sometimes, strangely, she would gently awaken me in the middle of the night just to lick me lovingly for a few seconds and then return to sleep at my feet. I, of course, interpreted this act of tenderness as a sign of my imminent death. (The newspapers said a friend of Callahan's mentioned his wiener dog kissed him the night before the bus crushed him to death in his wheelchair right in front of a group of cheering feminists!)

As unsinkable as Weenie was she did have her "Achilles' heel." My cat, Stanley, would wickedly hide in the irises and make a slight rustling sound. Weenie would then investigate by sticking her long and sensitive nose into the irises whereupon the cat would strike, sending Weenie weeping in agony down the sidewalk. She <u>fell</u> for it every time. Also, Weenie was weird. She would always go crazy and bark herself into a frenzy whenever she heard the voice of Paul

Drake, the private detective on the old TV show "Perry Mason."

Weenie died two years ago of an infection that came out of nowhere. Jerry Jeff Walker's song "Mr. Bojangles" tells us that his dog "up & died" and that after twenty years "he still grieves." I can relate to that! (It's bad enough when your dog dies, but that upping part is even harder to take!) This book of dog cartoons is dedicated to the memory of Weenie, my favorite dog.

John Callahan

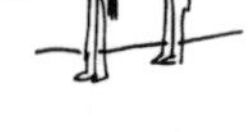

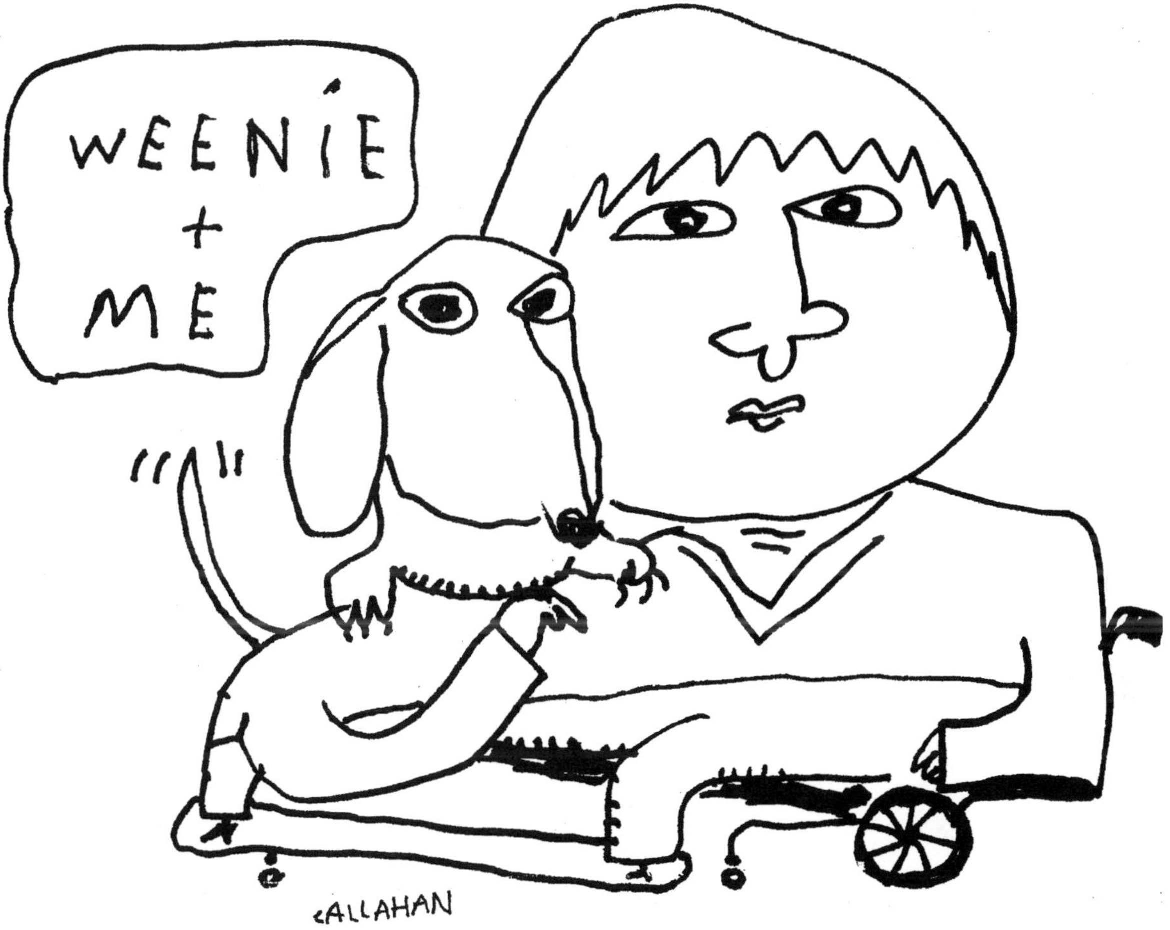
WEENIE + ME
CALLAHAN

10

...MY GOD!!! WHAT DOES THE DOG WANT?!

by

CALLAHAN

SOMETIMES I NOTICE
THE DOG
STARING AT ME!!!!!!!

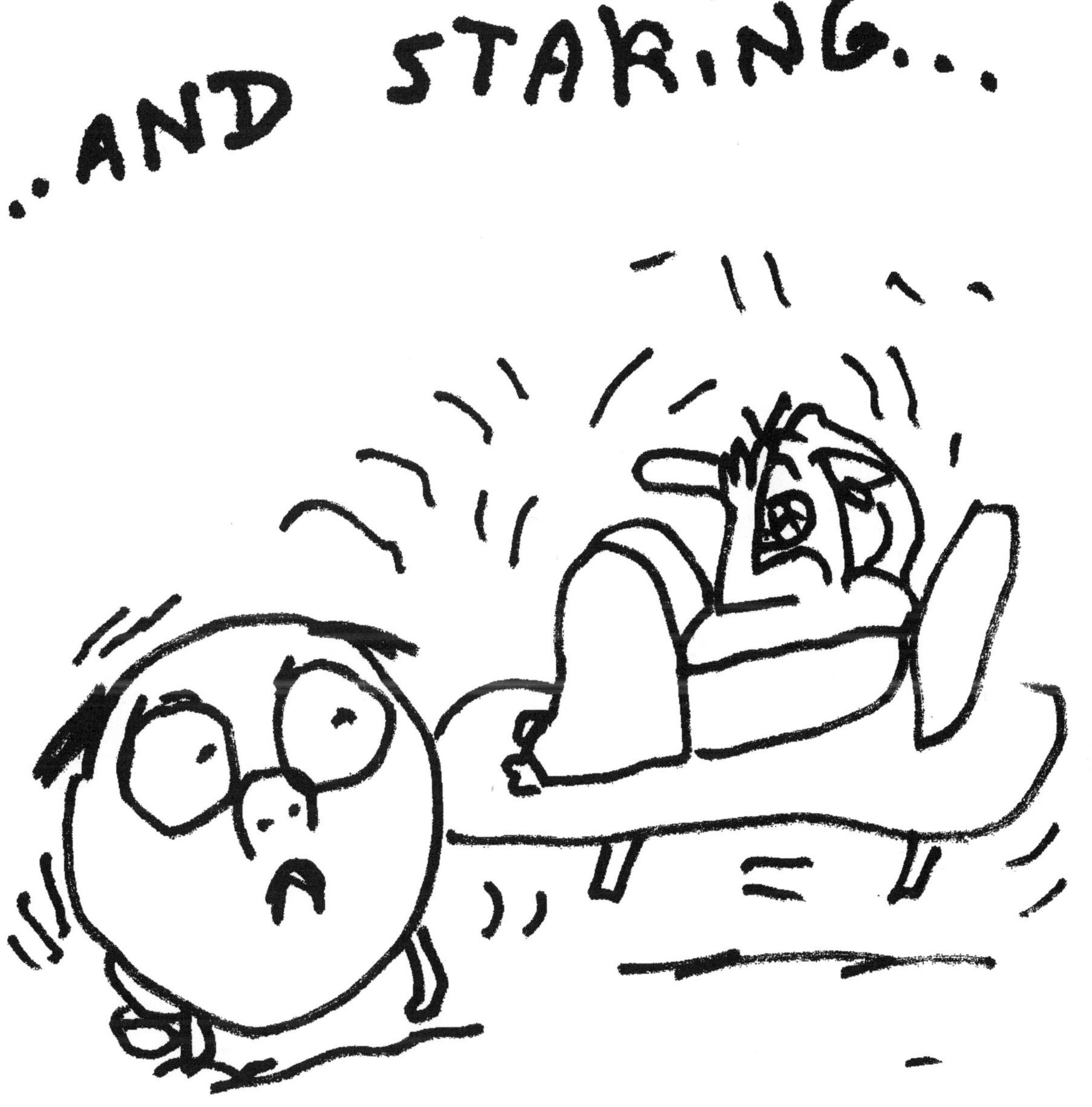
..AND STARING...

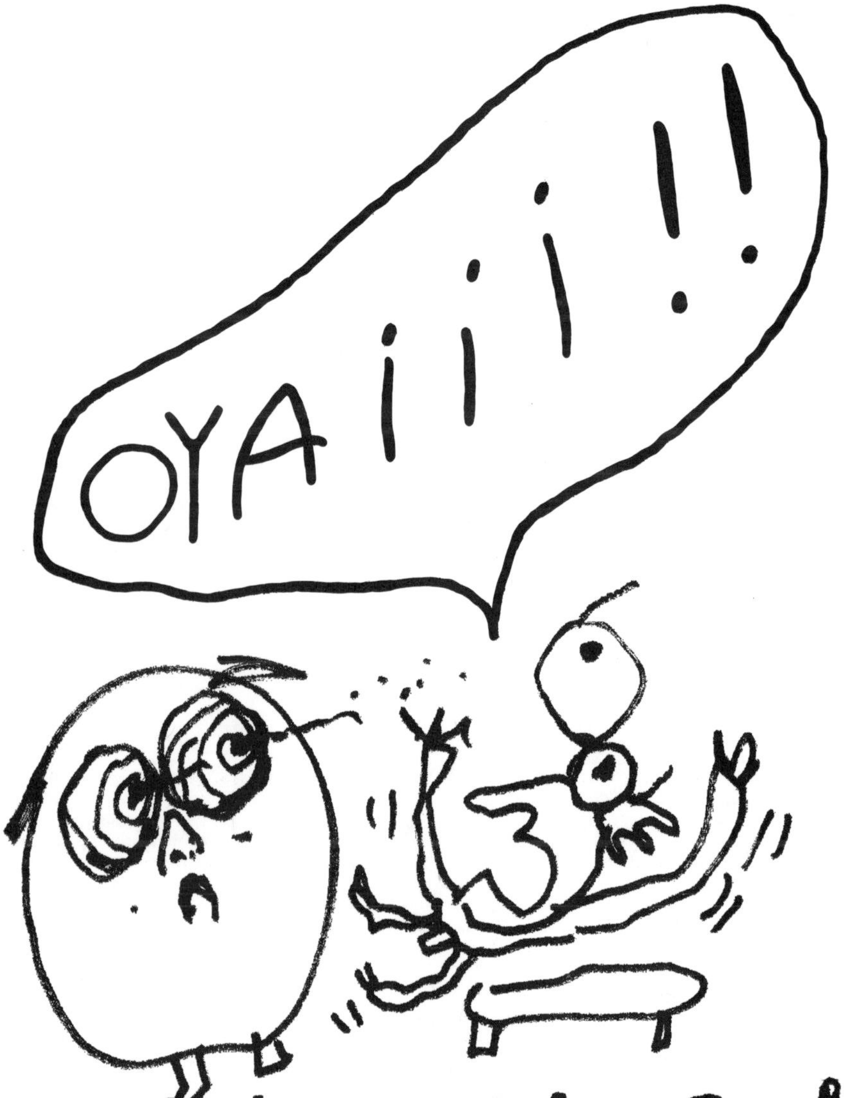
OYAiii!!

..AND STARING..!

...MY GOD!!! WHAT DOES THE DOG **WANT**?!

THE DOG is
TRYING TO
WEAR ME
DOWN...

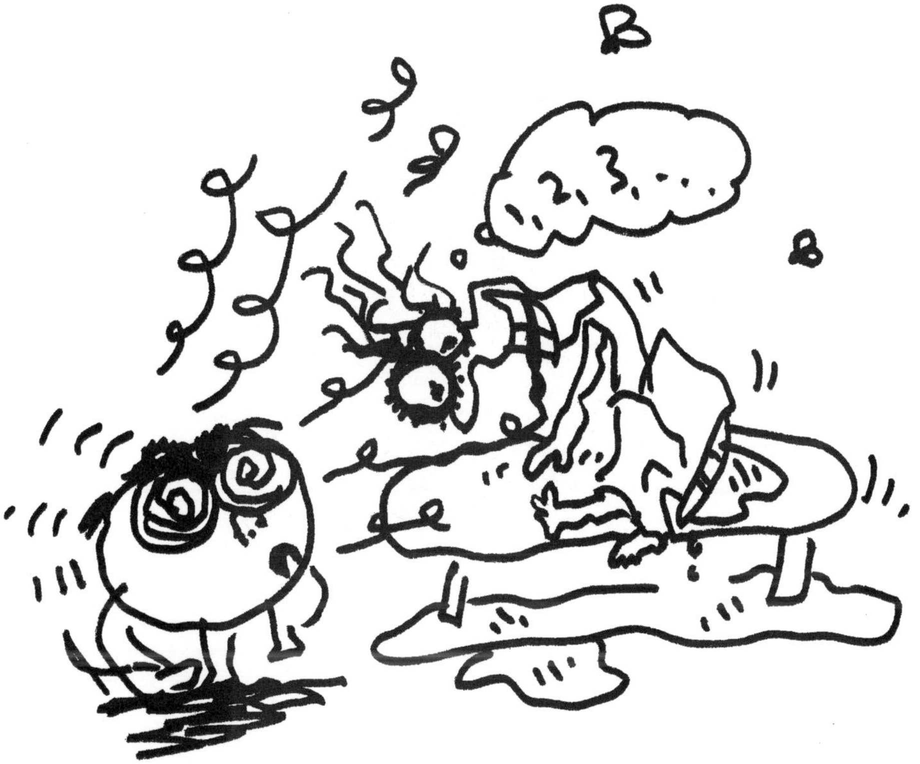
B
1, 2, 3, . . .
B

. . . TO BREAK ME DOWN. . . .

THE DOG KNOWS SOMETHING I DON'T...

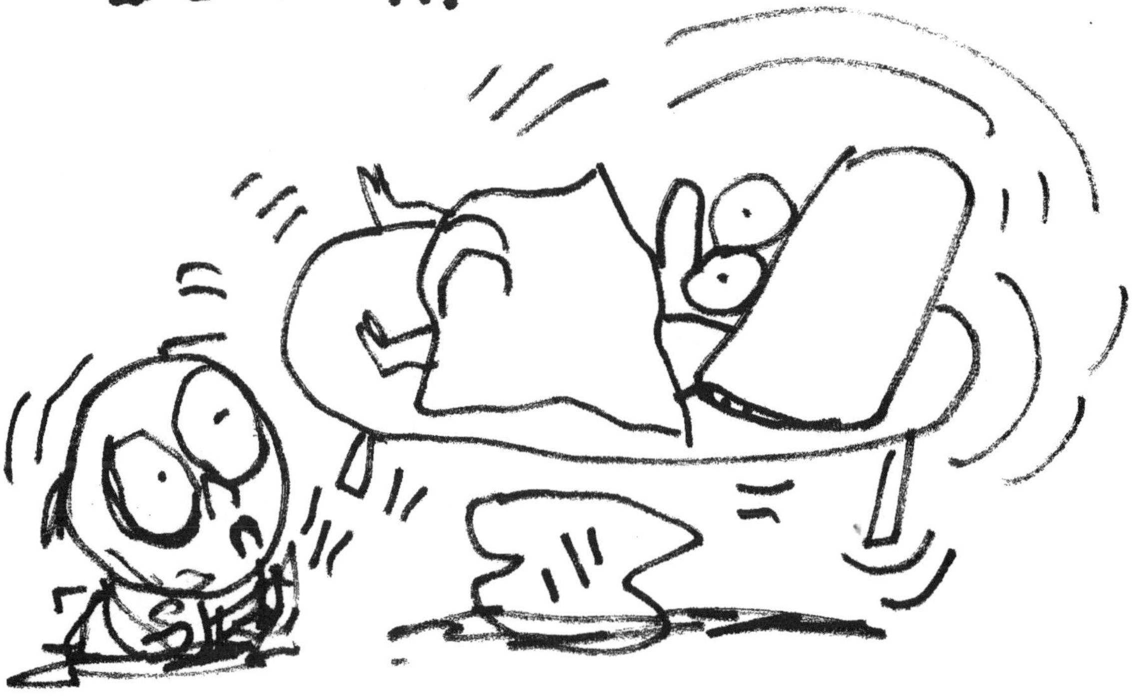

..PERHAPS THE DOG THINKS I'M A HOMOSEXUAL.

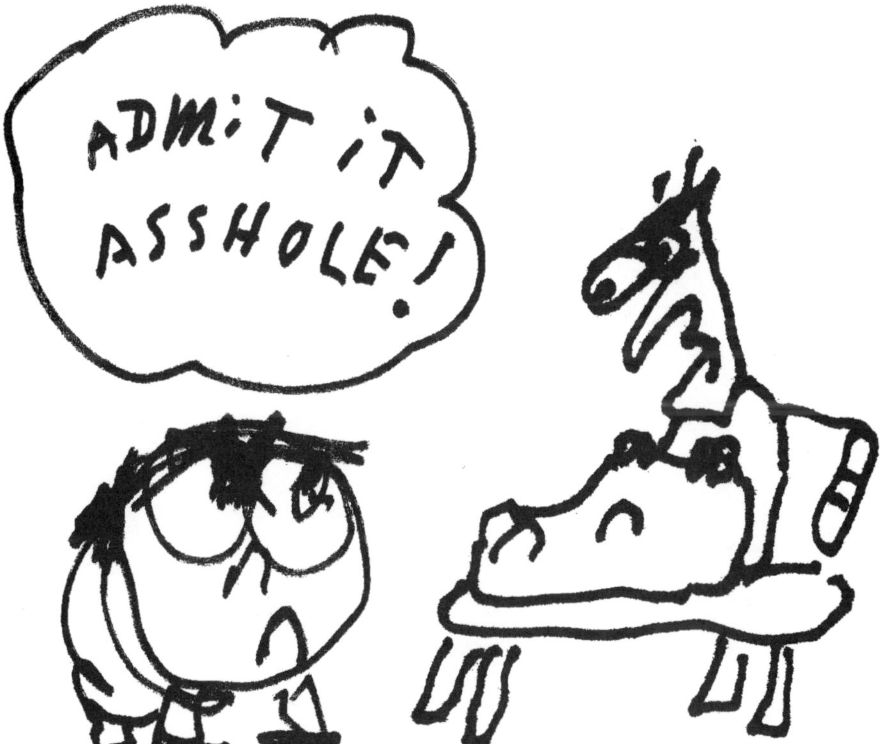
ADMIT IT ASSHOLE!

THE DOG WANTS ME TO BE HONEST AND DEAL WITH THIS PART OF MY LIFE...

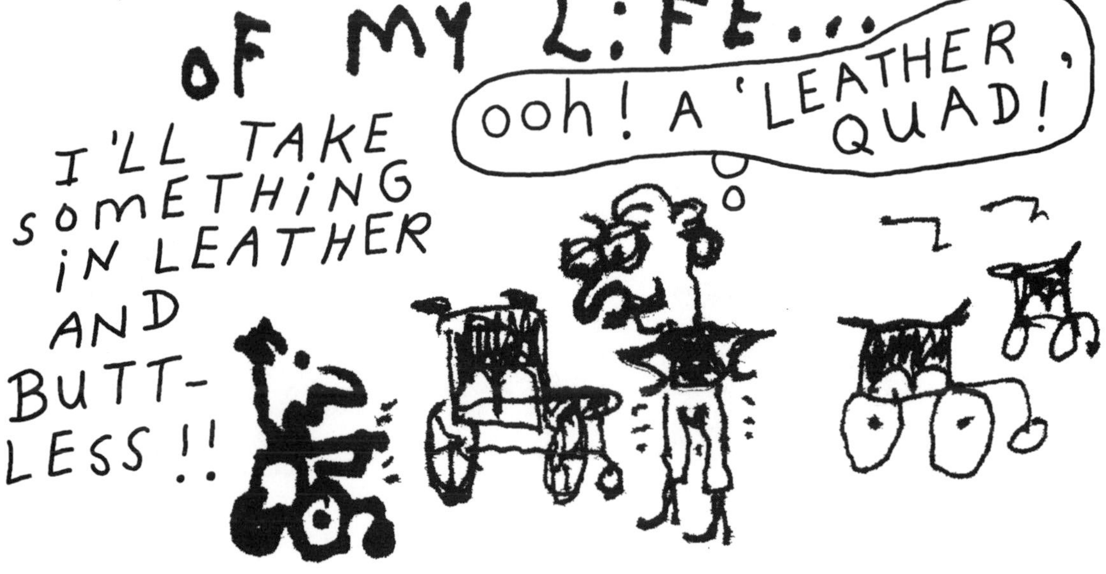
I'LL TAKE SOMETHING iN LEATHER AND BUTT-LESS!!
ooh! A 'LEATHER QUAD!'

PERHAPS HE THINKS I'M NOT REALLY PARALYZED...

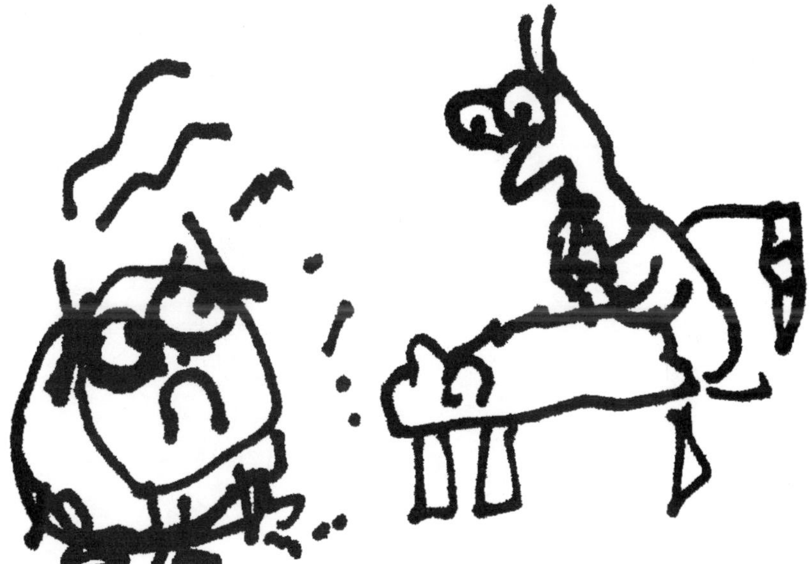

THE DOG IS TRYING TO CONVEY THAT I'M ONLY <u>CONVINCED</u> I'M DISABLED DUE TO AN 'HYSTERICAL REACTION' BROUGHT ABOUT BY STRESS AND TRAUMA...

...THAT I COULD HAVE MISINTERPRETED THE PROGNOSIS...

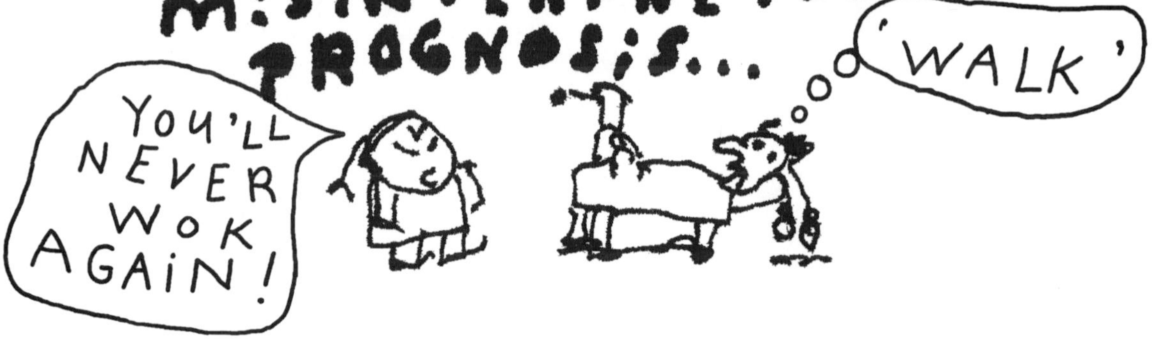
YOU'LL NEVER WOK AGAIN!
'WALK'

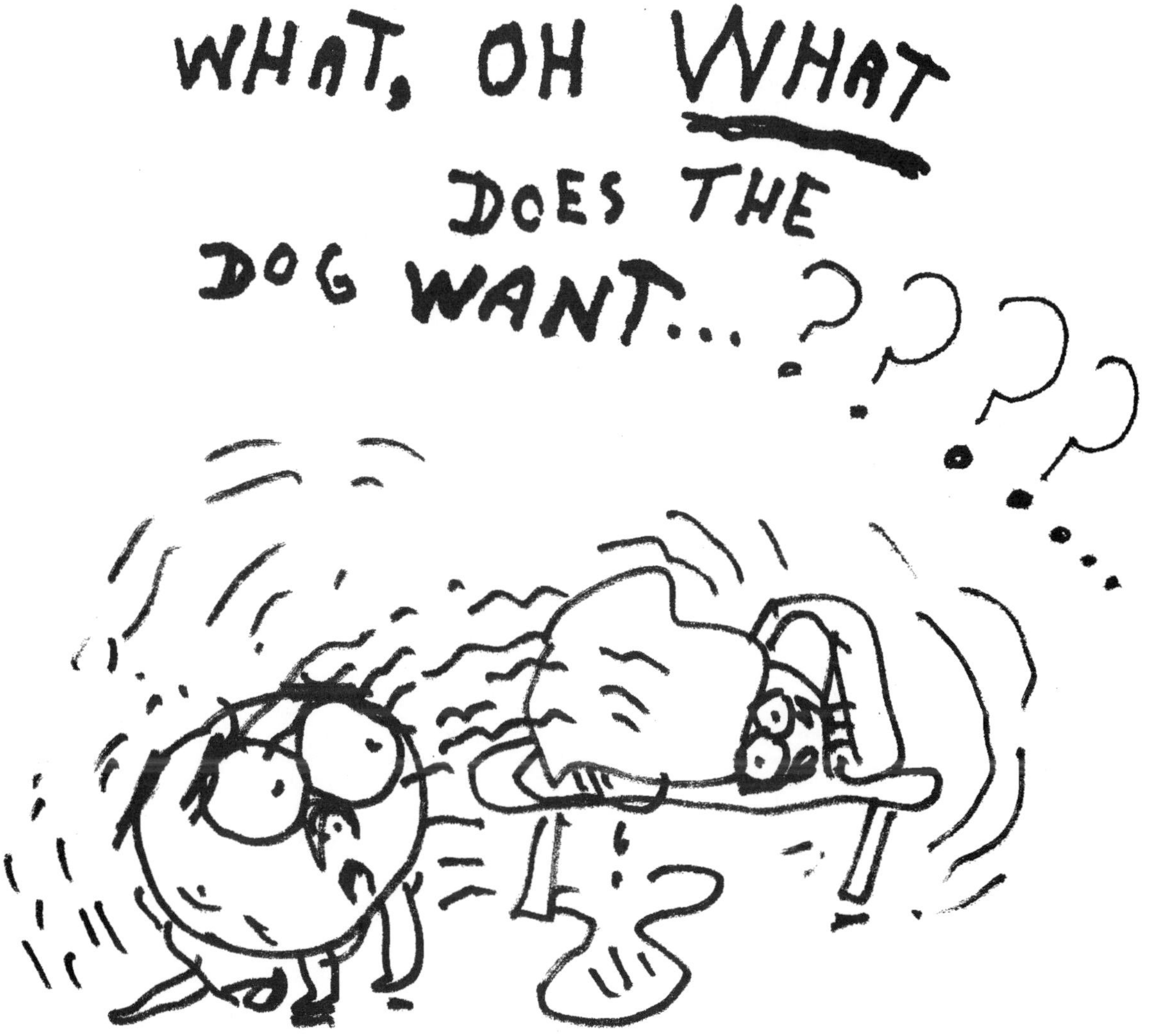
WHAT, OH WHAT DOES THE DOG WANT...???

FINALLY MY AIDE
DISCLOSES THE ANSWER...

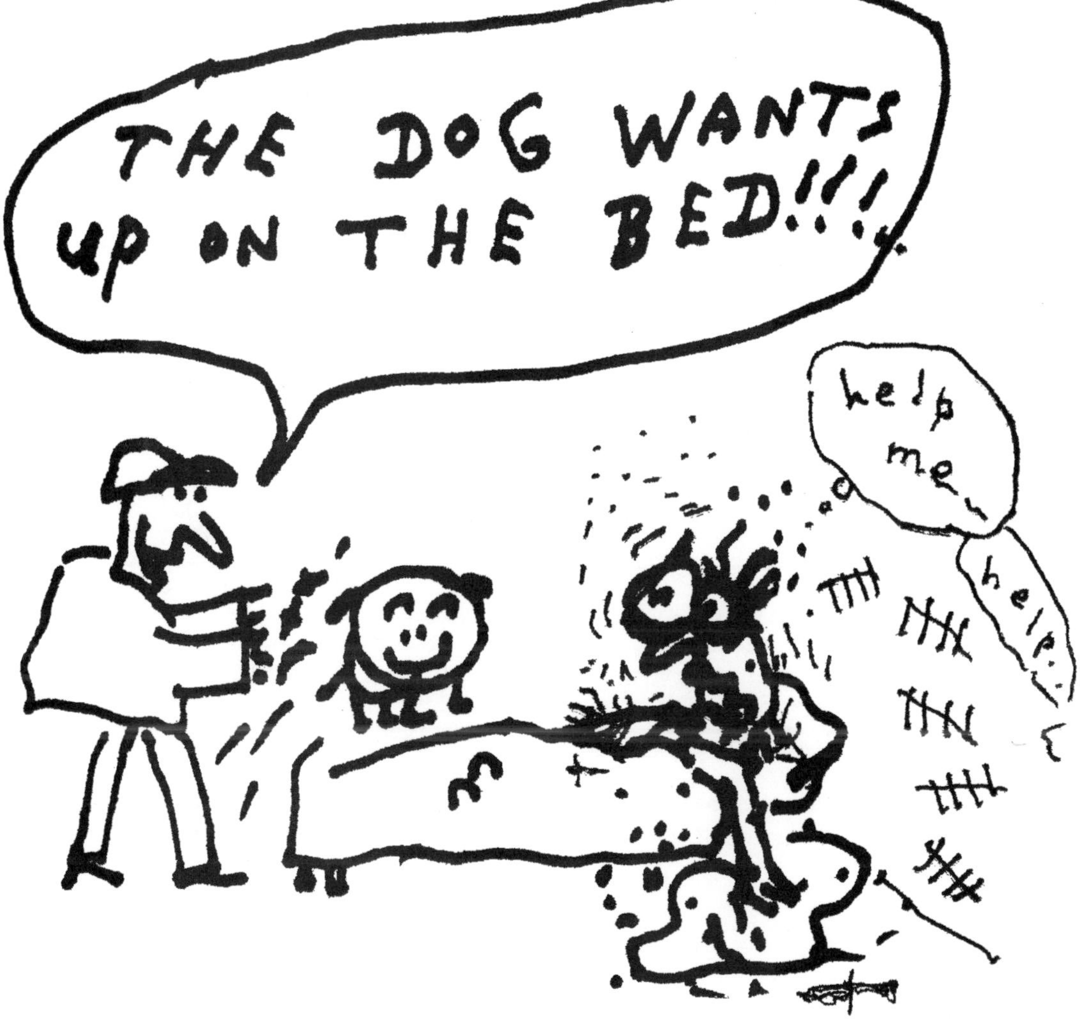
THE DOG WANTS UP ON THE BED!!!!
help me
help

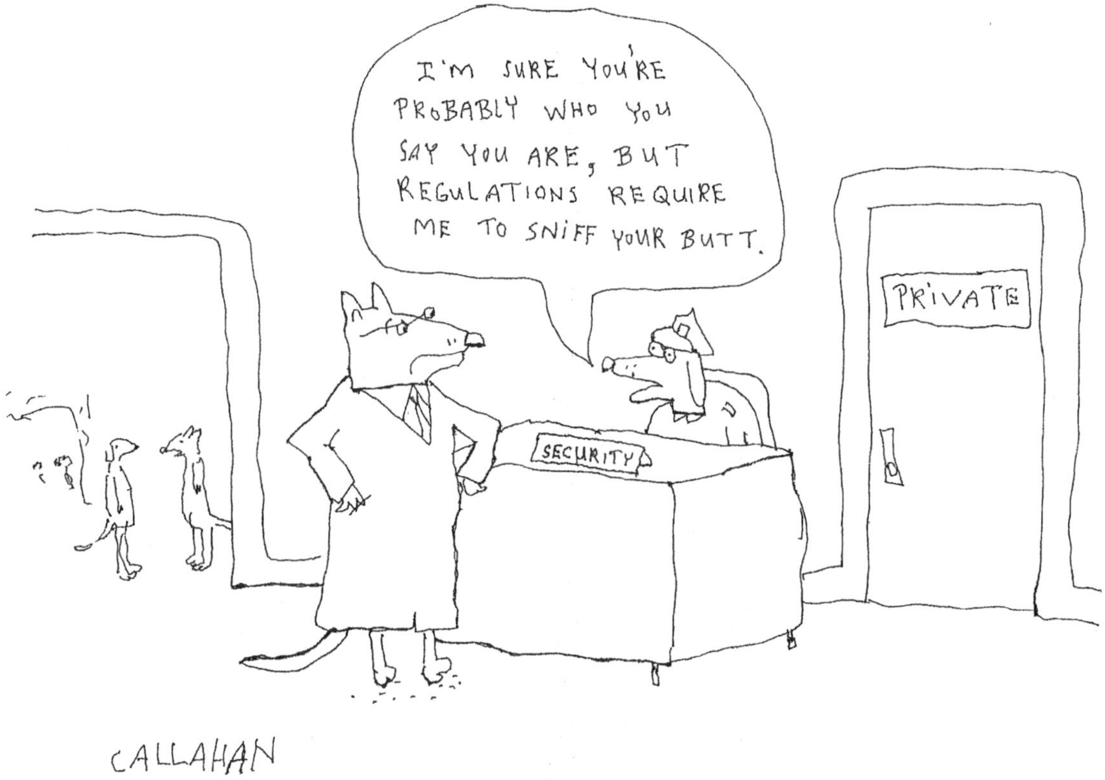
I'M SURE YOU'RE PROBABLY WHO YOU SAY YOU ARE, BUT REGULATIONS REQUIRE ME TO SNIFF YOUR BUTT.
SECURITY
PRIVATE
CALLAHAN

HEY!! YOU KNEW I 'SCOOTED' WHEN YOU MARRIED ME!
CALLAHAN

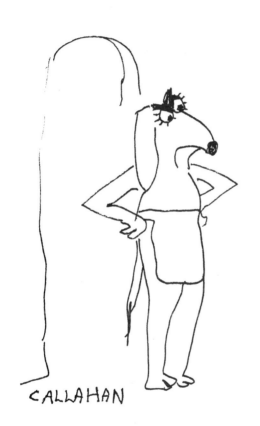

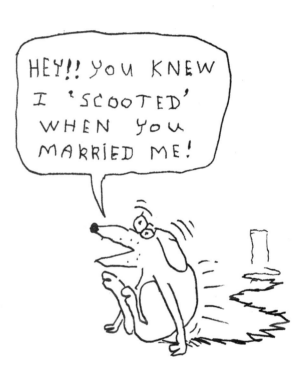

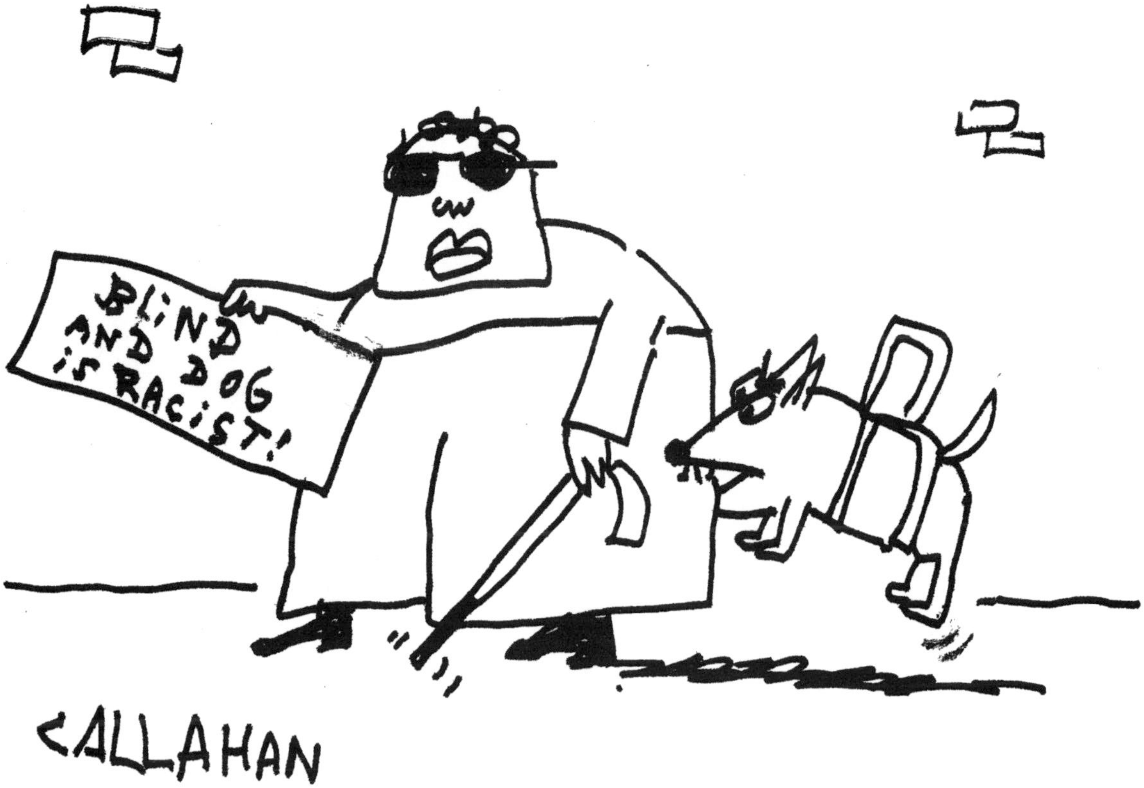
BLIND AND DOG IS RACIST!
CALLAHAN

CALLAHAN

29

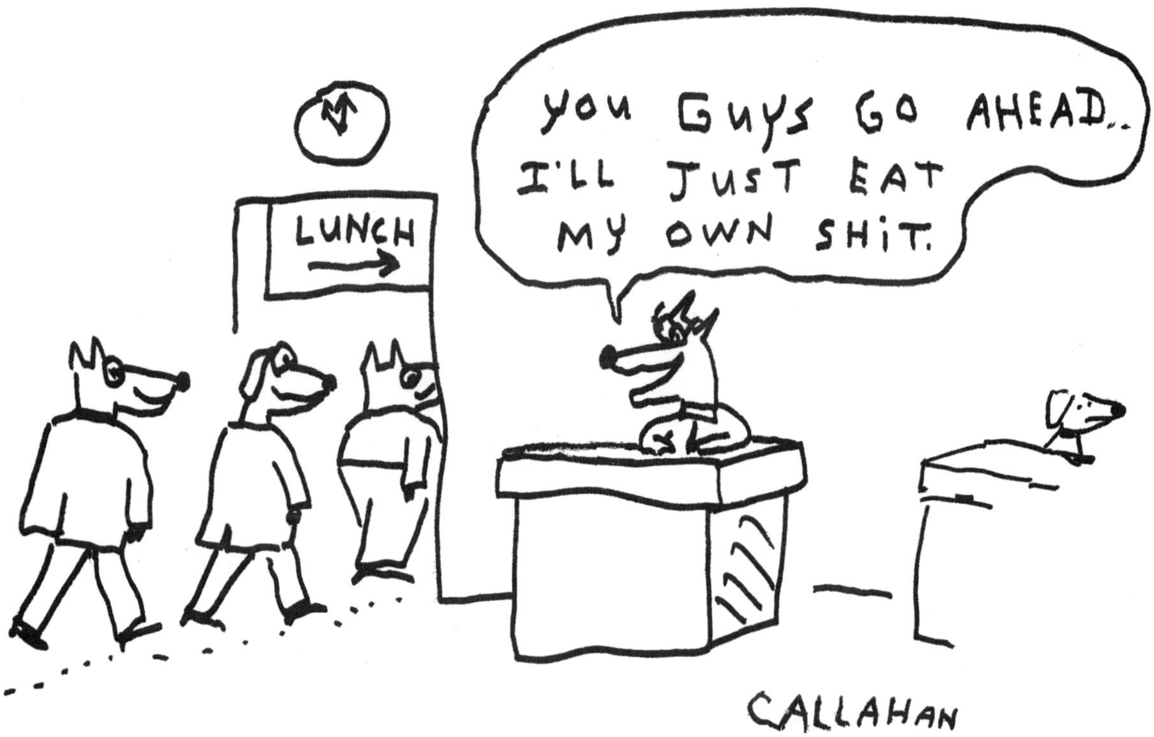
LUNCH
YOU GUYS GO AHEAD..
I'LL JUST EAT
MY OWN SHIT.
CALLAHAN

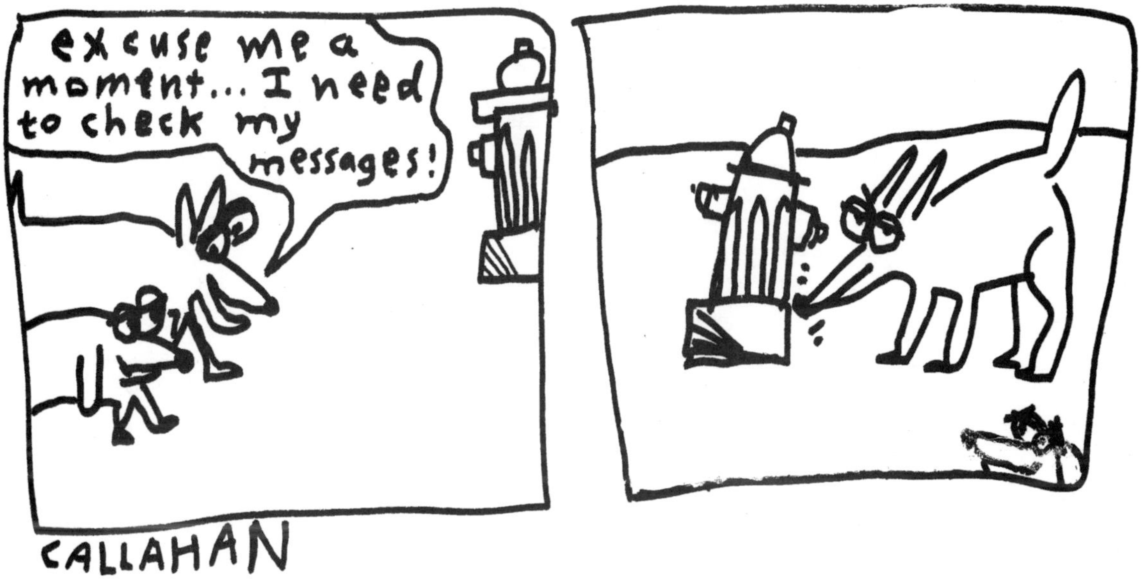
excuse me a moment... I need to check my messages!
CALLAHAN

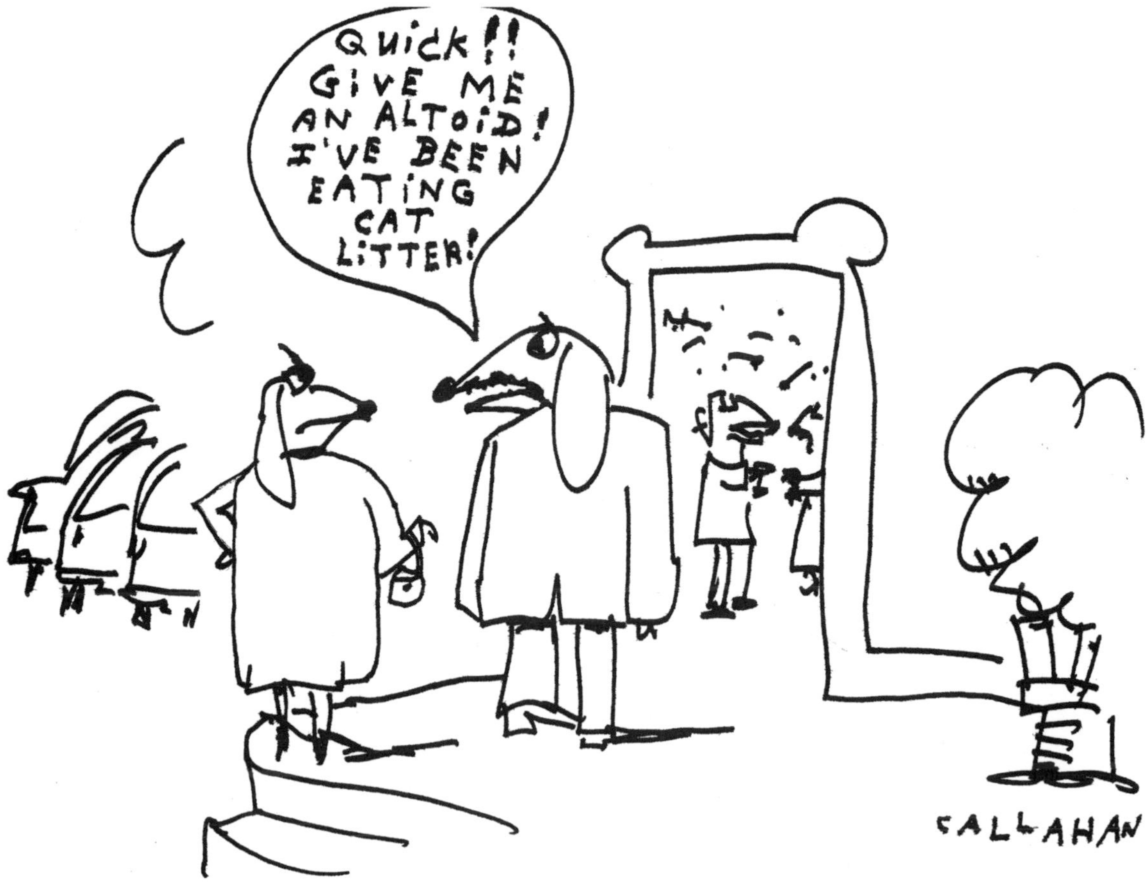
QUICK!! GIVE ME AN ALTOID! I'VE BEEN EATING CAT LITTER!
CALLAHAN

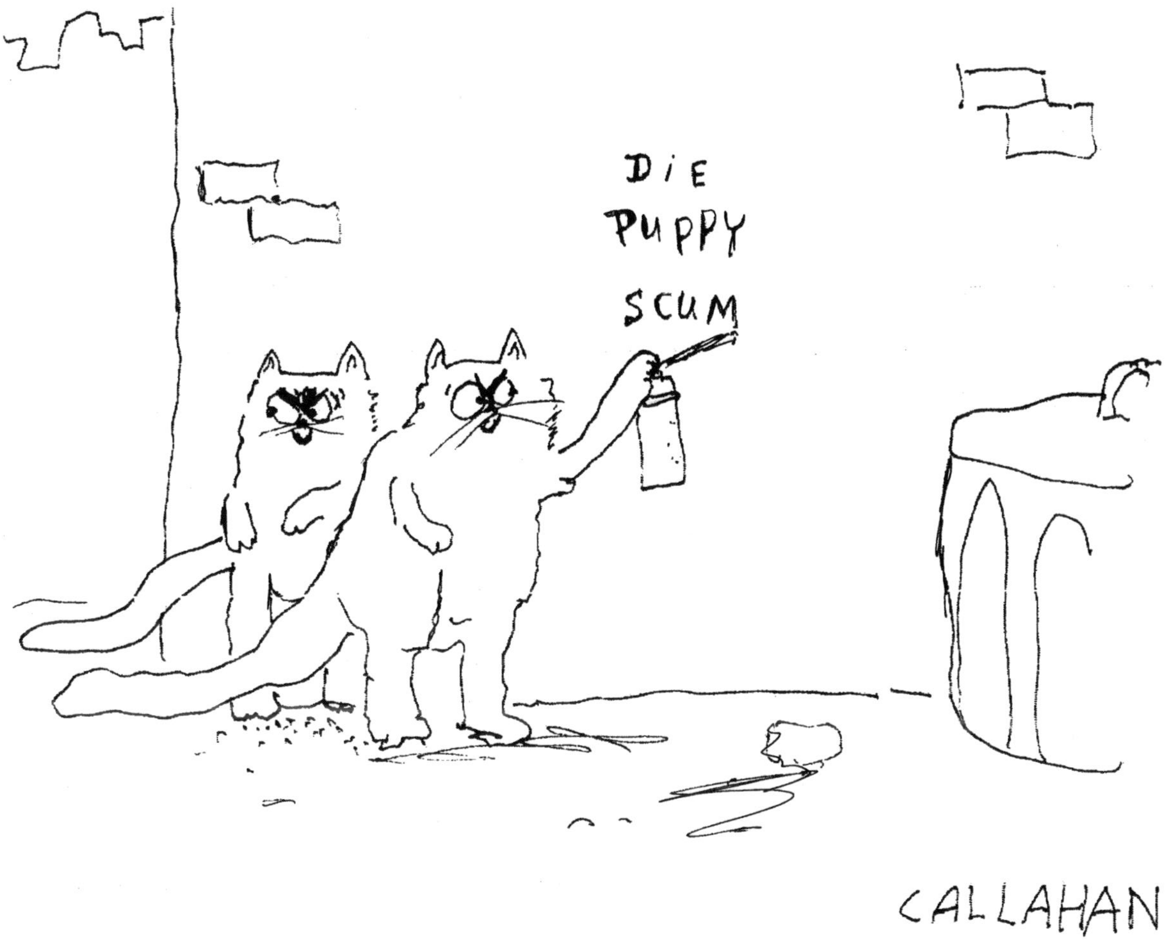
DIE
PUPPY
SCUM
CALLAHAN

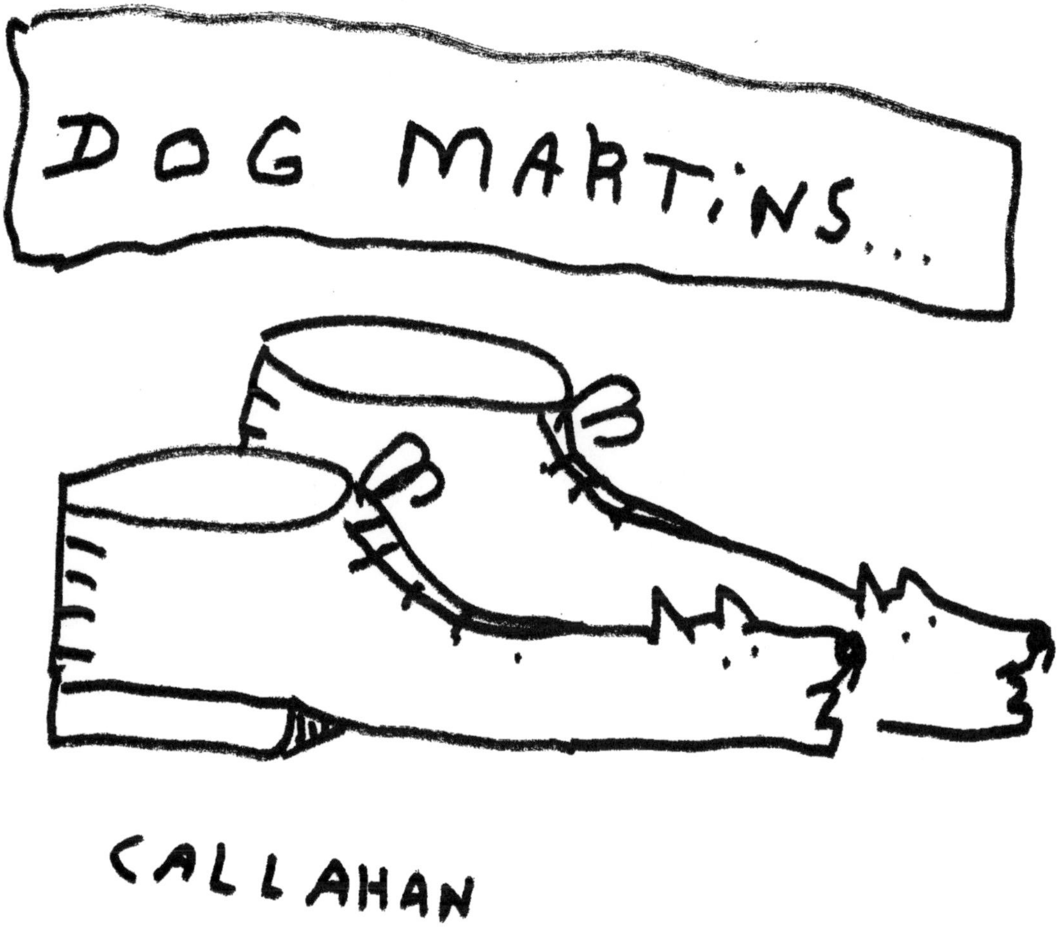
DOG MARTINS...
CALLAHAN

DOG PRACTICING TELE·KINESIS.

CALLAHAN

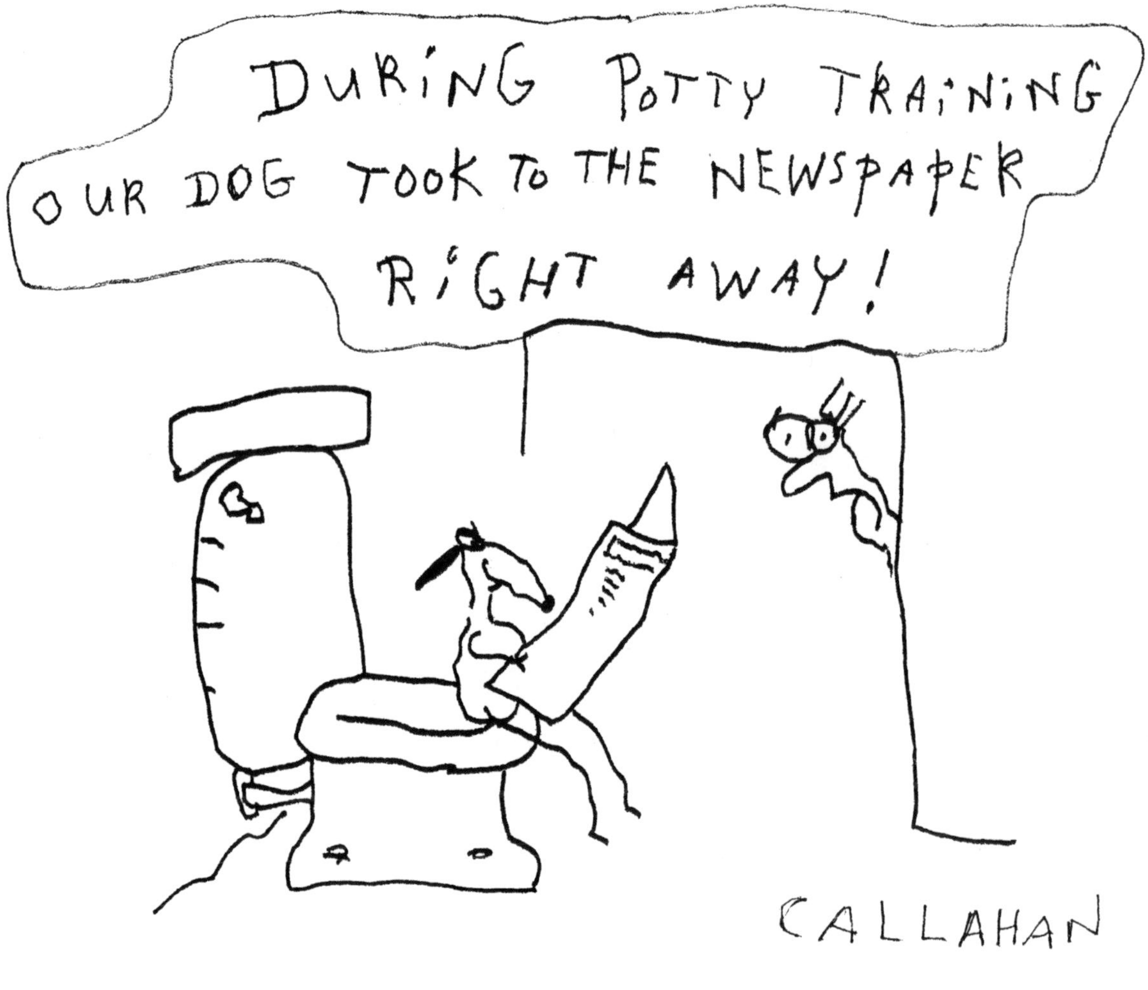
DURING POTTY TRAINING OUR DOG TOOK TO THE NEWSPAPER RIGHT AWAY!
CALLAHAN

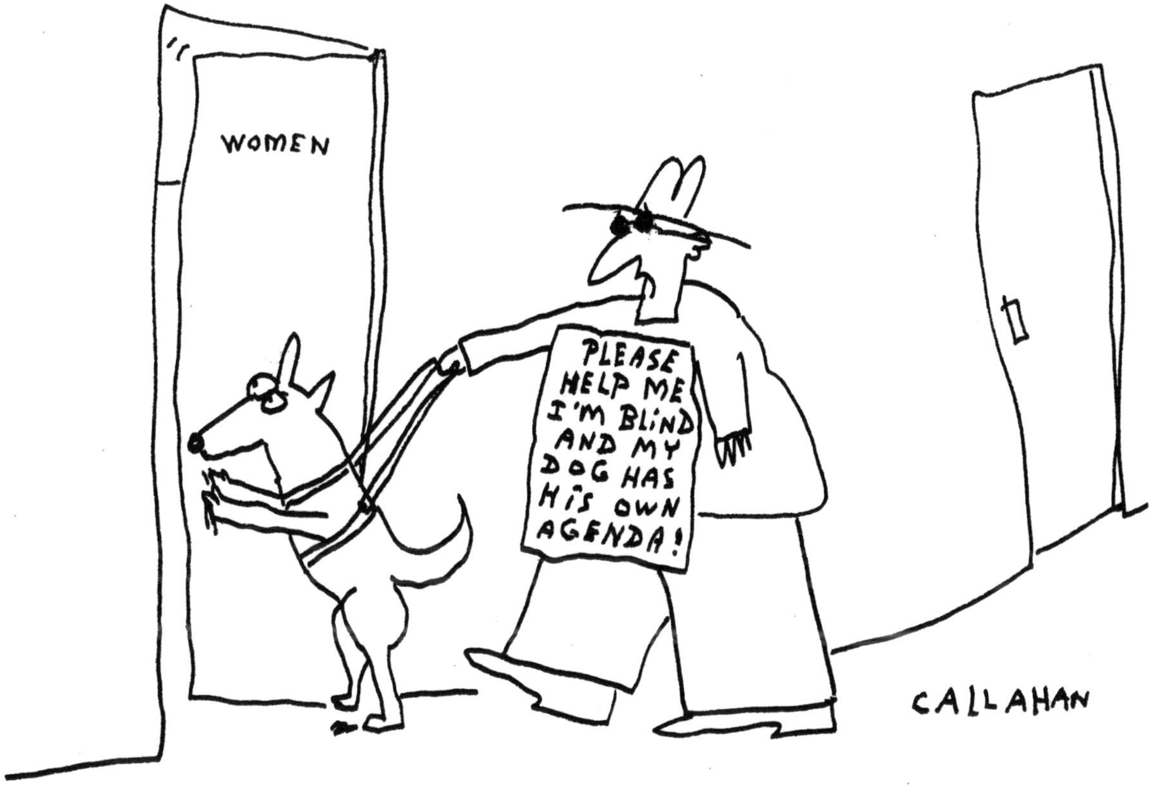
WOMEN
PLEASE HELP ME I'M BLIND AND MY DOG HAS HIS OWN AGENDA!
CALLAHAN

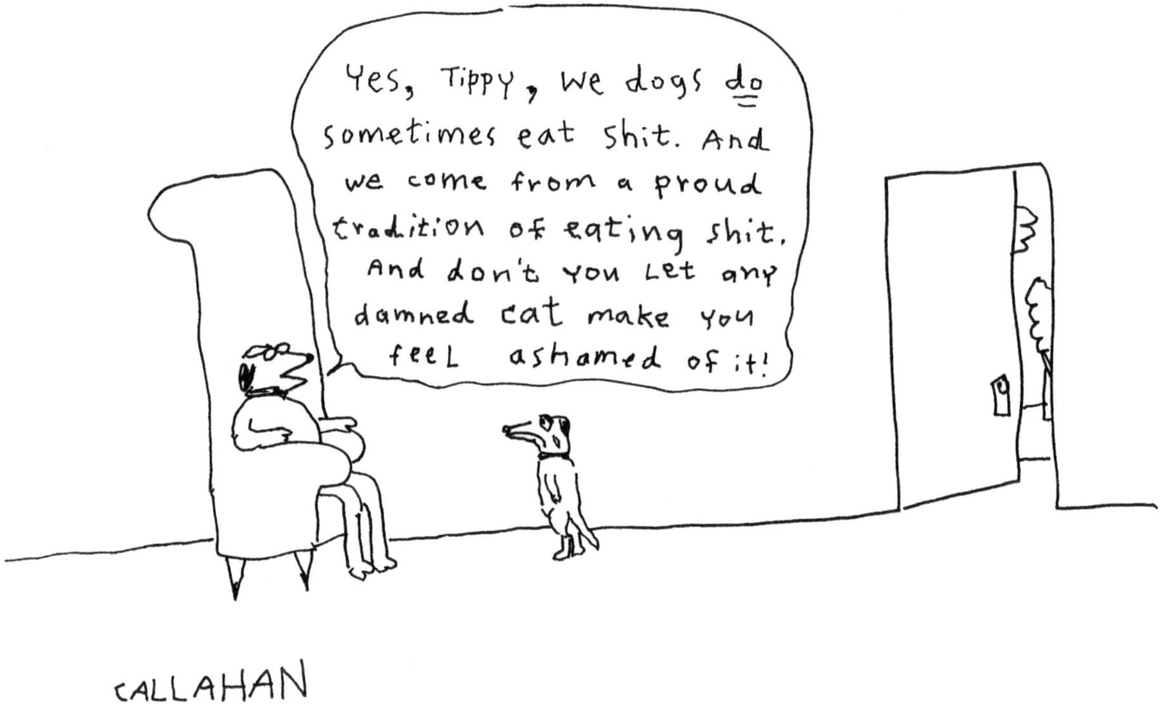
Yes, Tippy, we dogs do sometimes eat shit. And we come from a proud tradition of eating shit. And don't you let any damned cat make you feel ashamed of it!
CALLAHAN

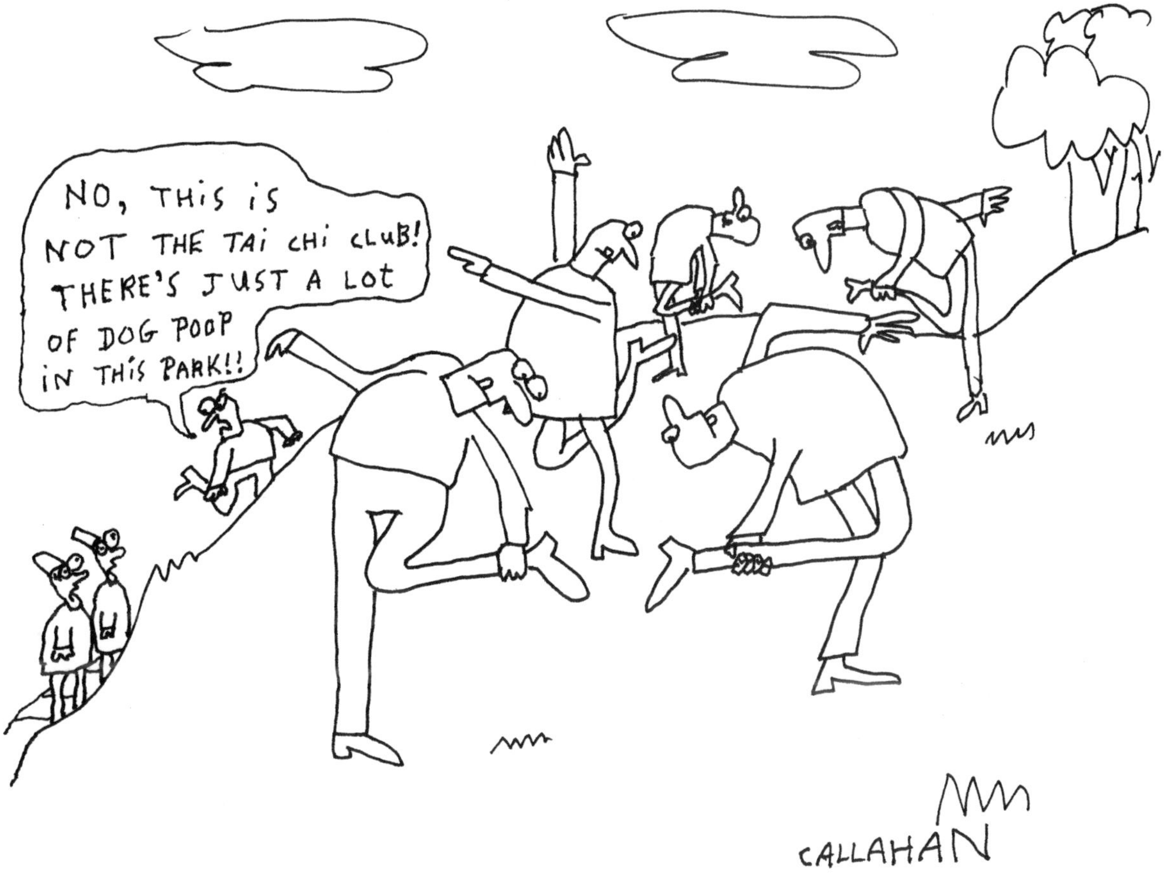
NO, THIS IS NOT THE TAI CHI CLUB! THERE'S JUST A LOT OF DOG POOP IN THIS PARK!!
CALLAHAN

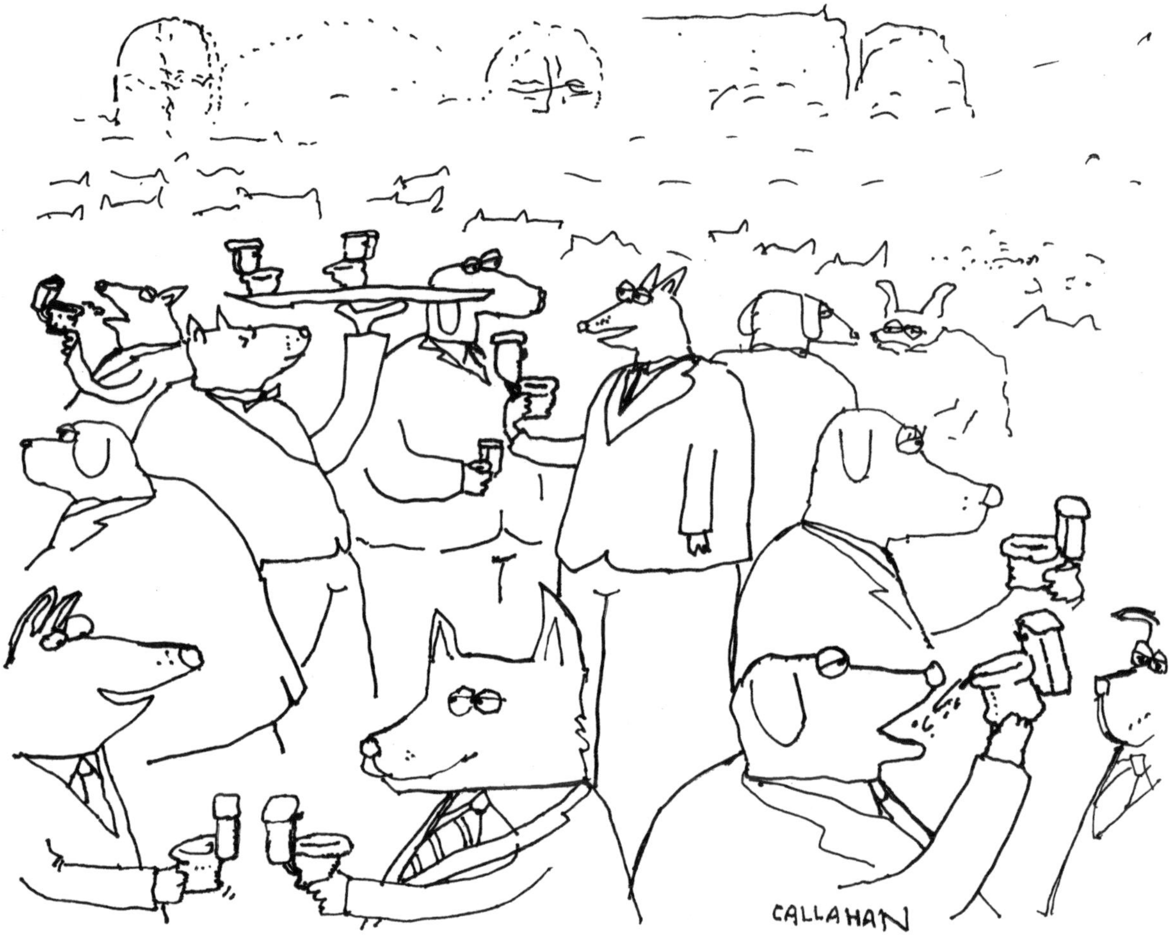
CALLAHAN

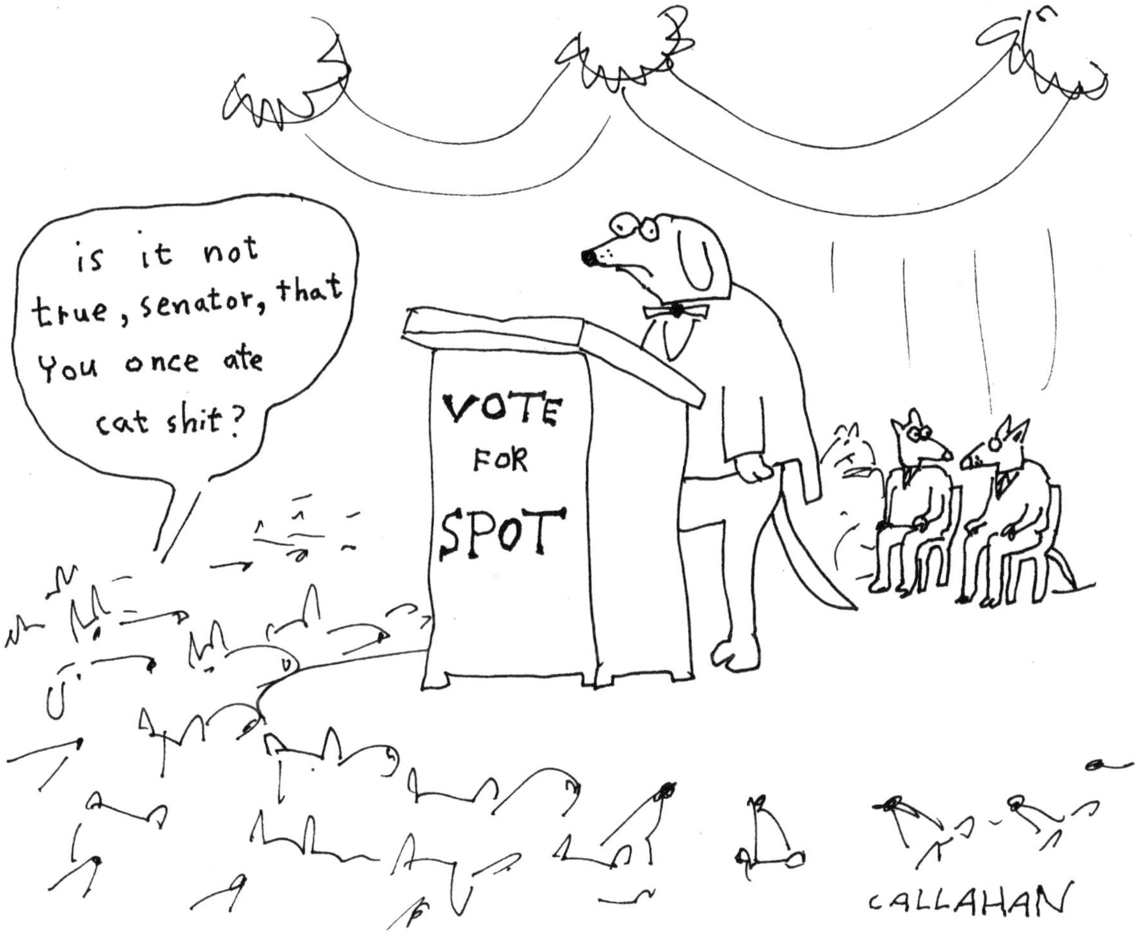
is it not true, senator, that you once ate cat shit?
VOTE FOR SPOT
CALLAHAN

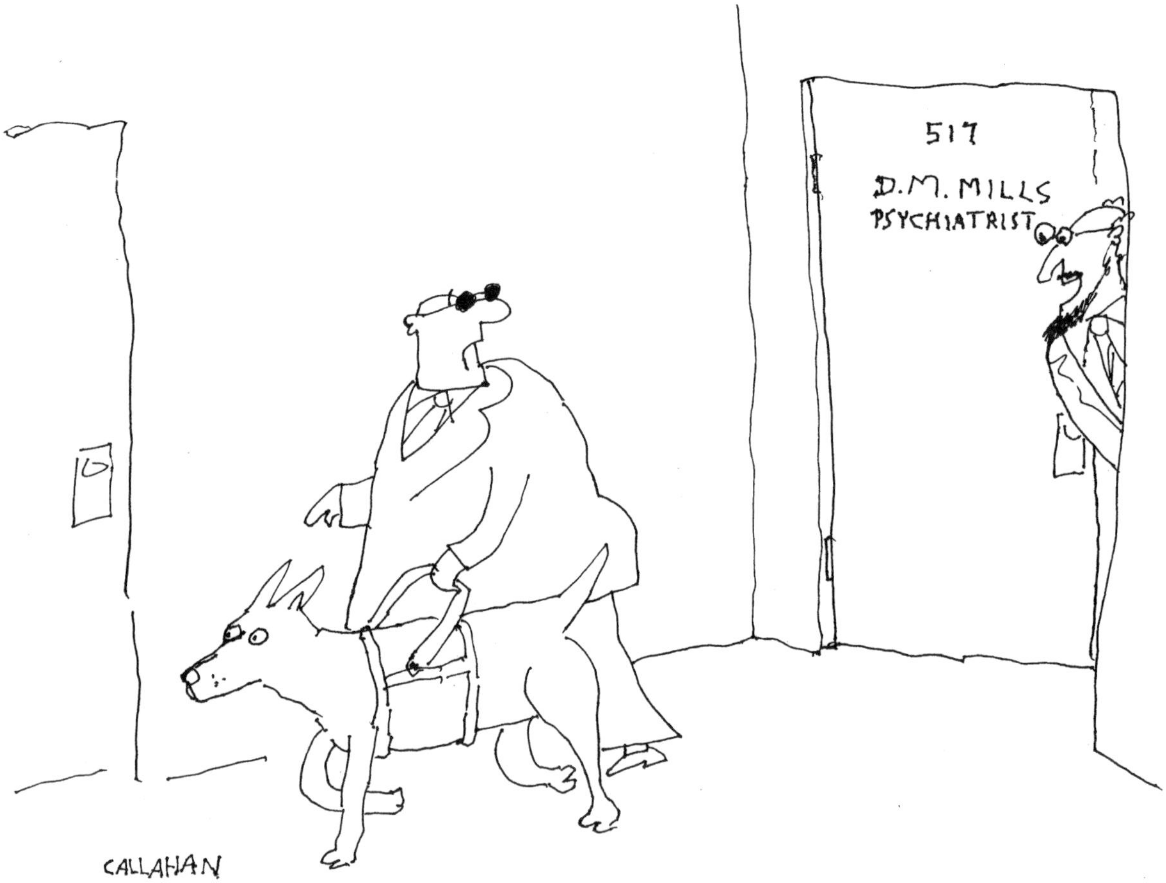
517
D.M. MILLS
PSYCHIATRIST
CALLAHAN

"Be sure to give Sparky three tranquilizers a day for your hallucinations."

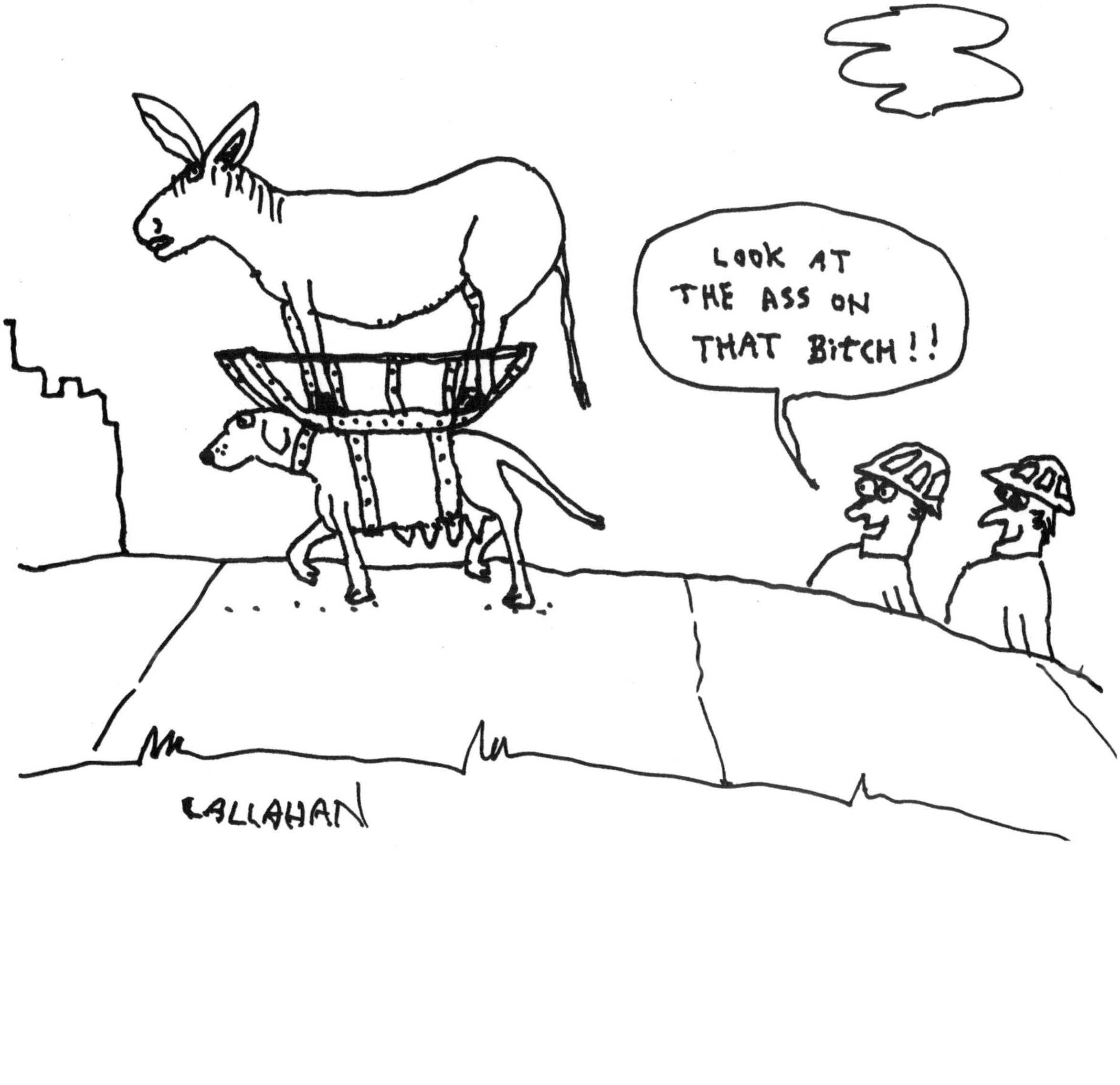
LOOK AT THE ASS ON THAT BITCH!!
CALLAHAN

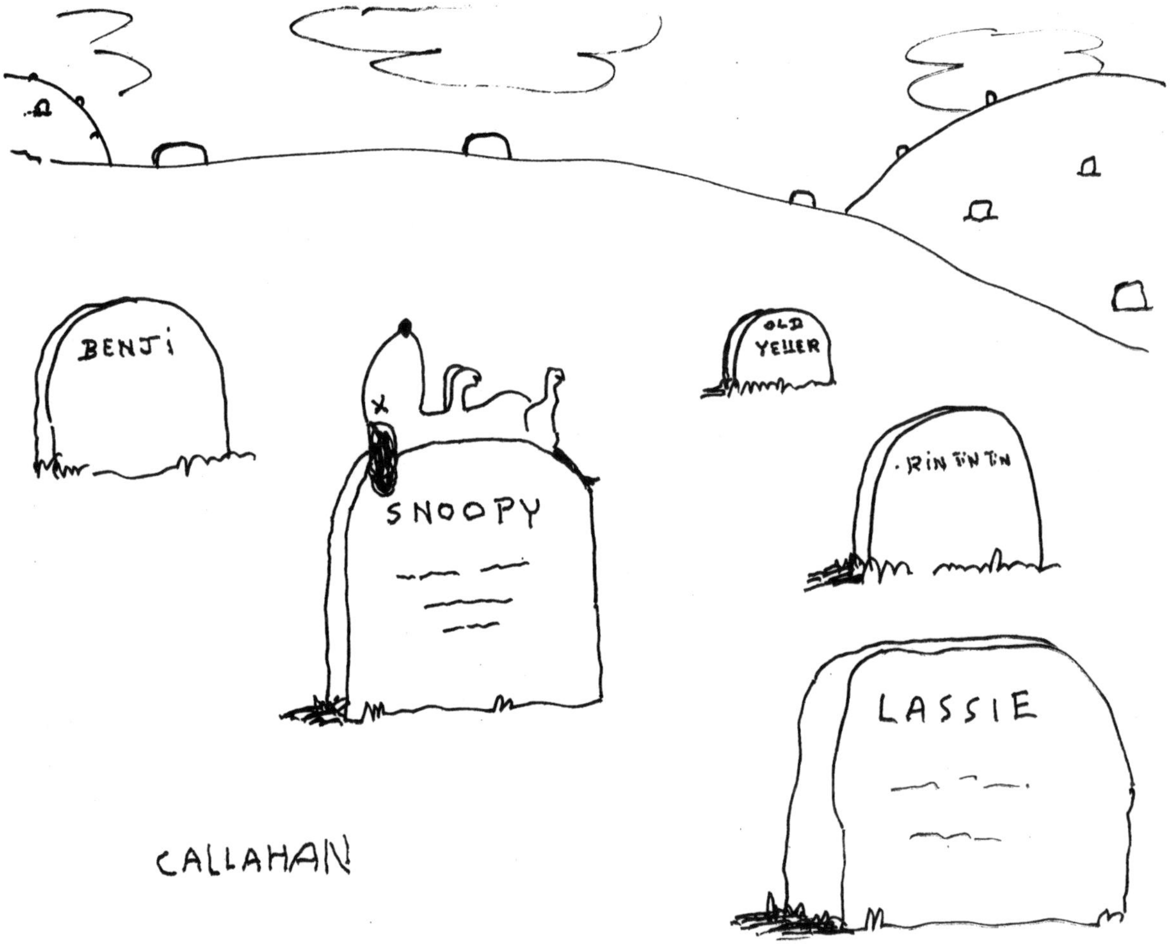
BENJI
SNOOPY
OLD YELLER
RIN TIN TIN
LASSIE
CALLAHAN

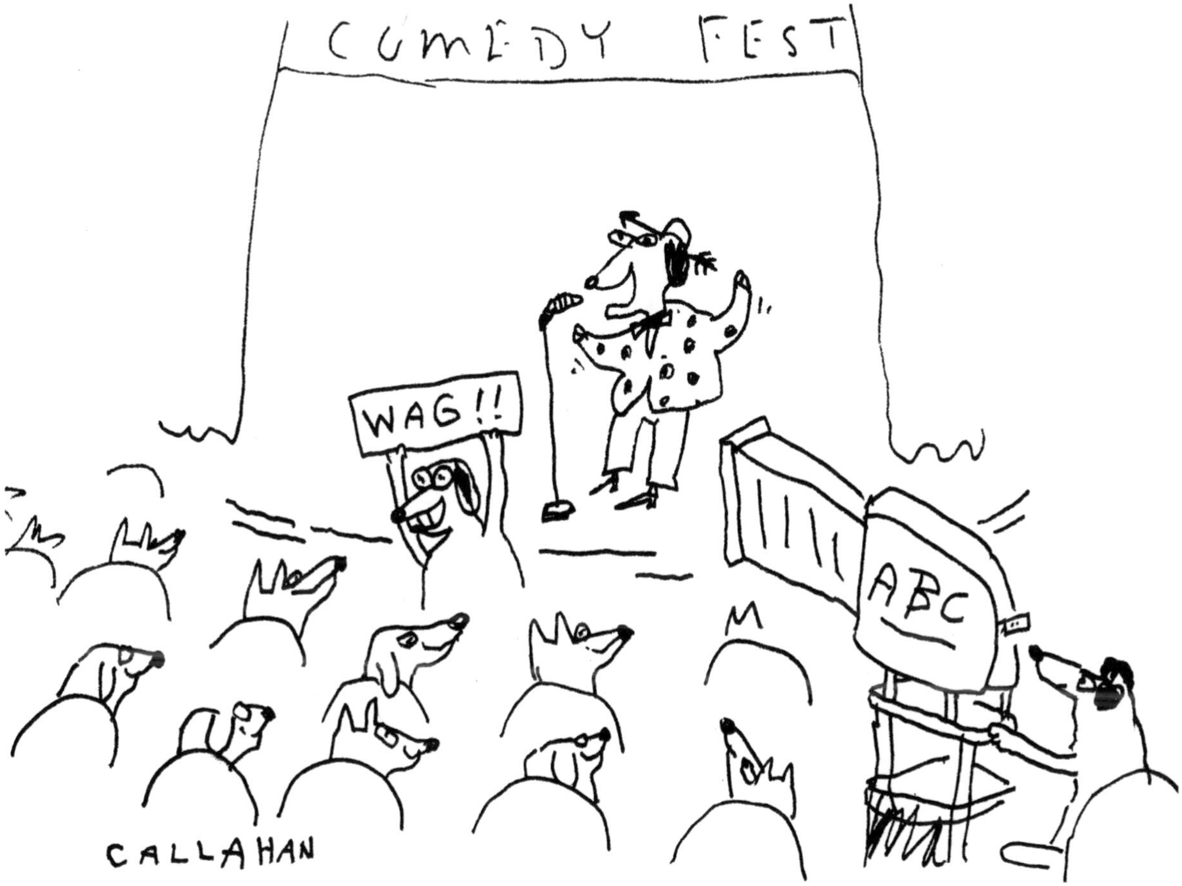
COMEDY FEST
WAG!!
ABC
CALLAHAN

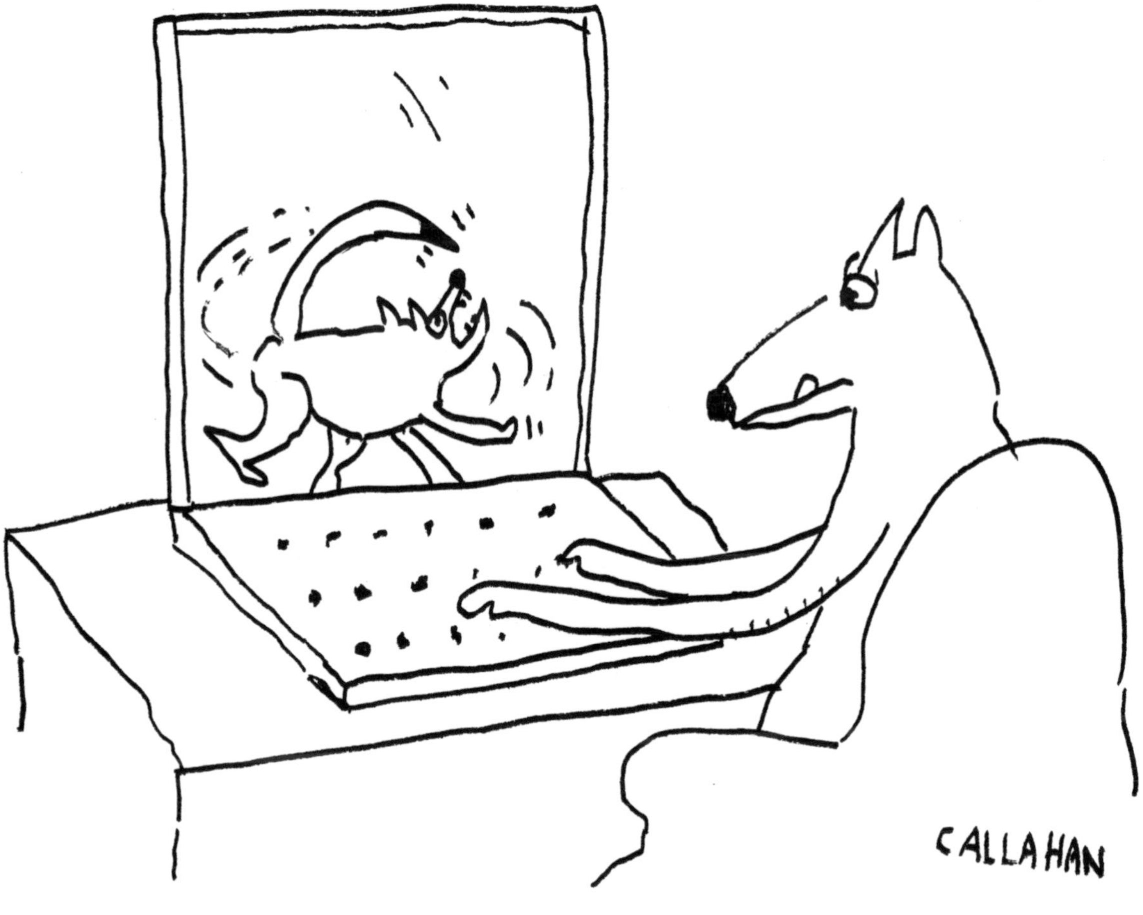
CALLAHAN

GET DOWN!!
CALLAHAN

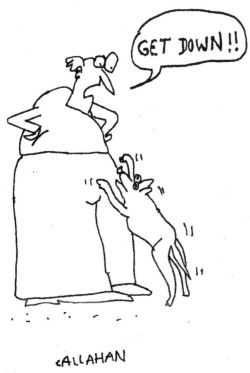

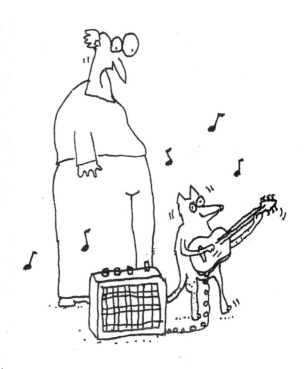

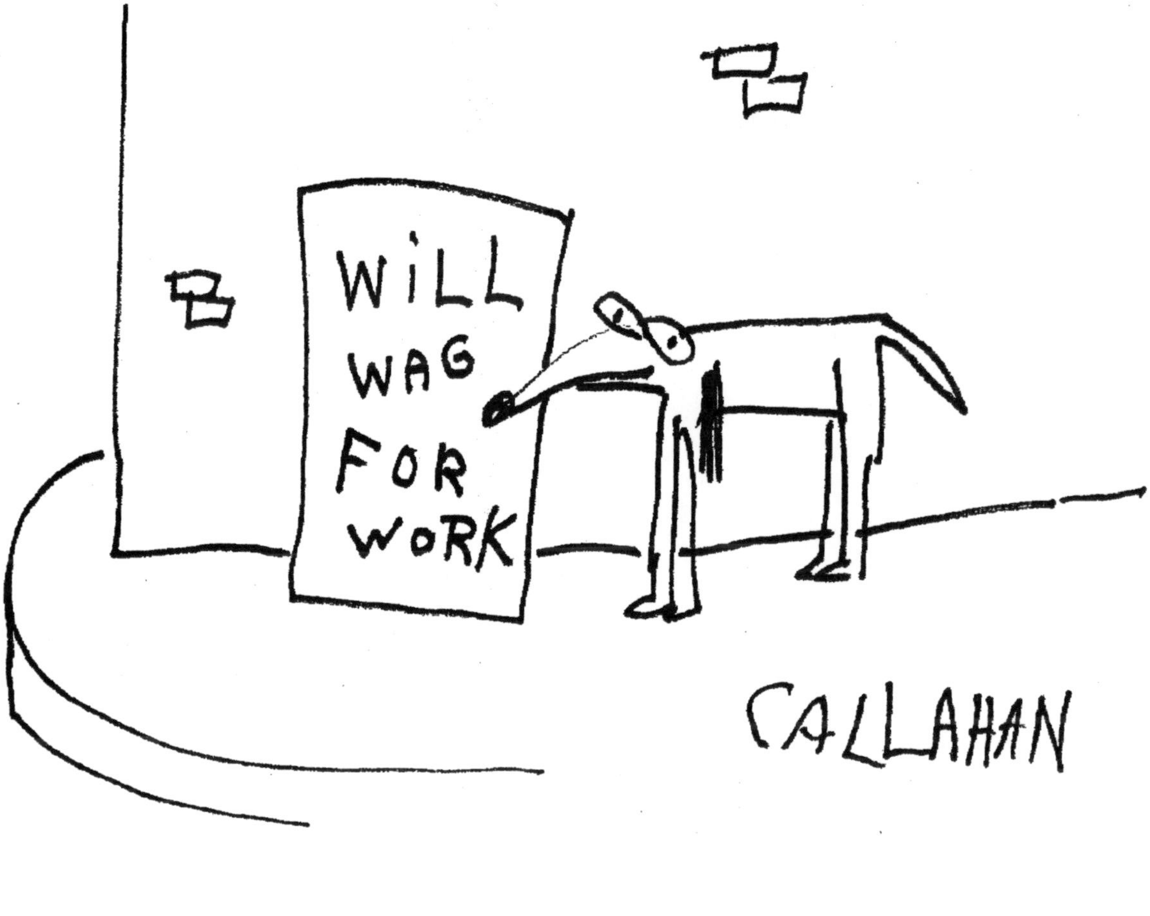
WILL
WAG
FOR
WORK
CALLAHAN

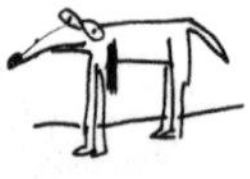

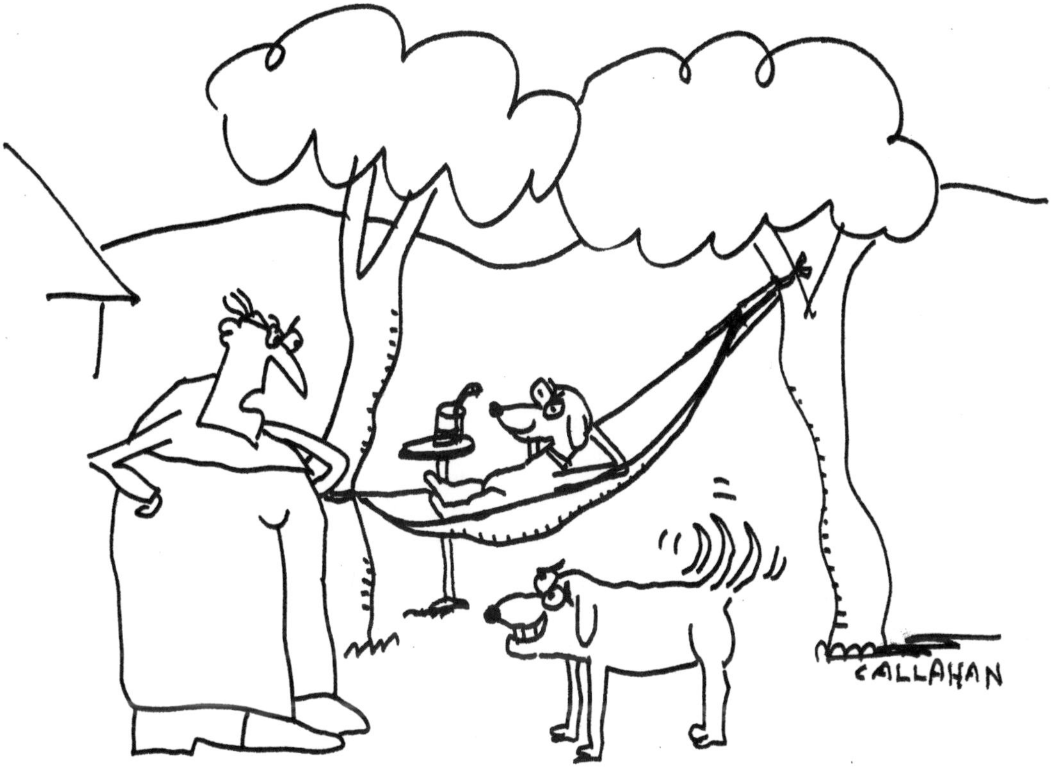
CALLAHAN

CALLAHAN

"You've got to be kidding... A 'designated wagger?'"

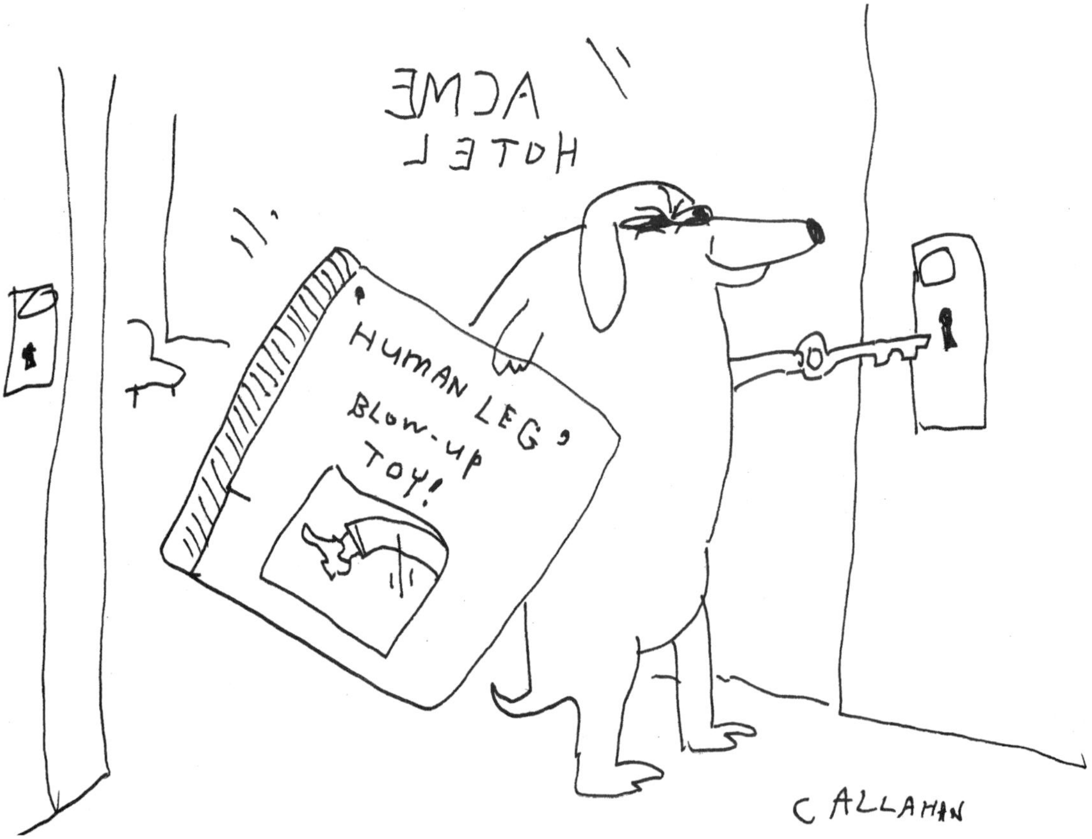
ACME
HOTEL
HUMAN LEG
BLOW-UP
TOY!
CALLAHAN

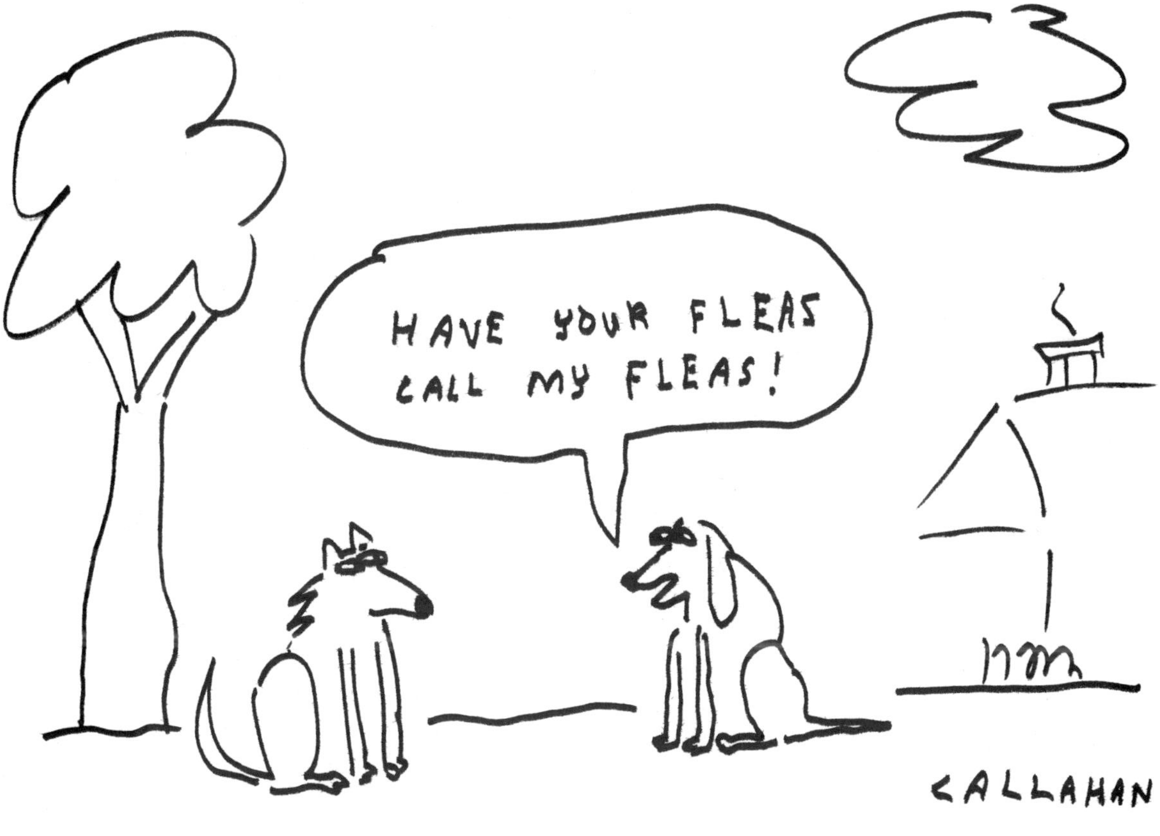
HAVE YOUR FLEAS CALL MY FLEAS!
CALLAHAN

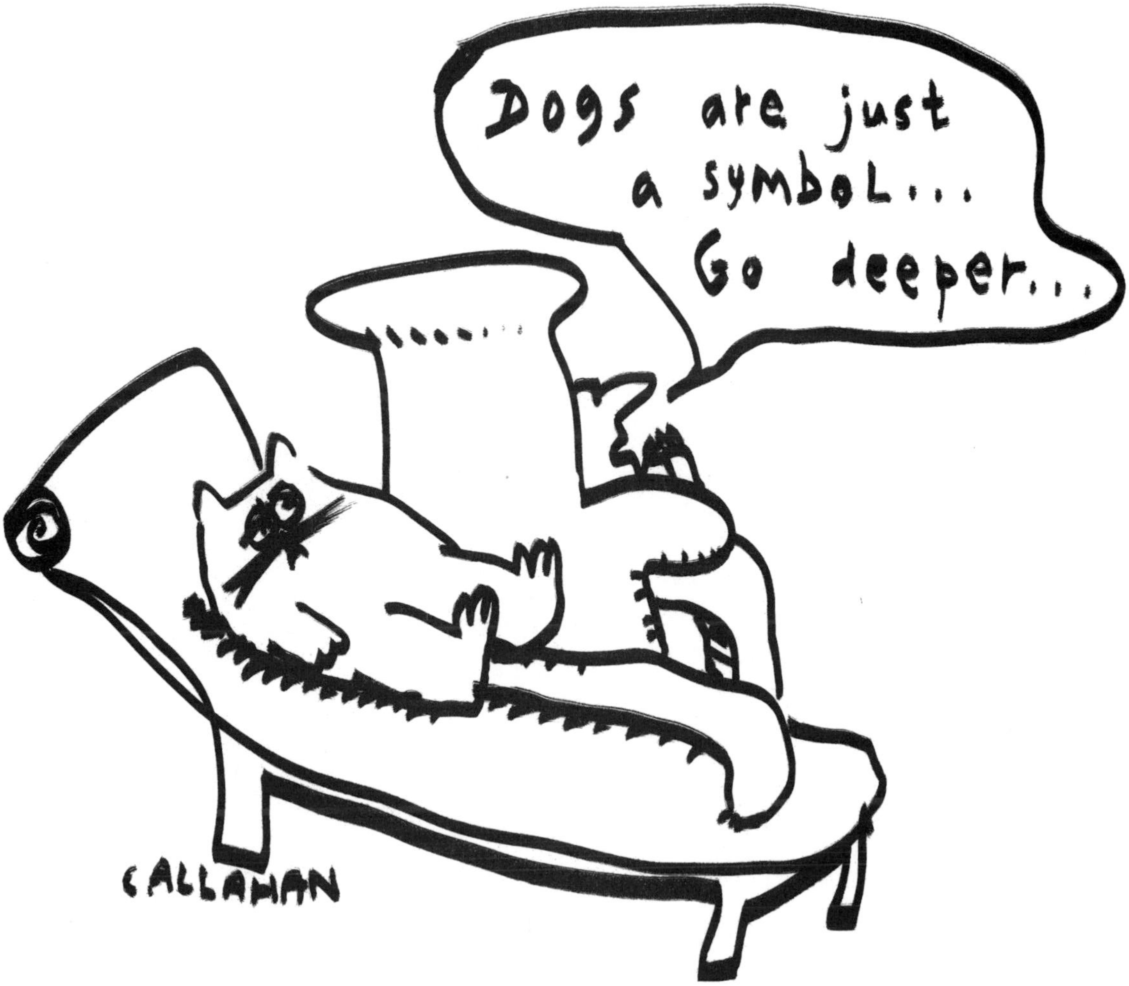
Dogs are just a symbol... Go deeper...
CALLAHAN

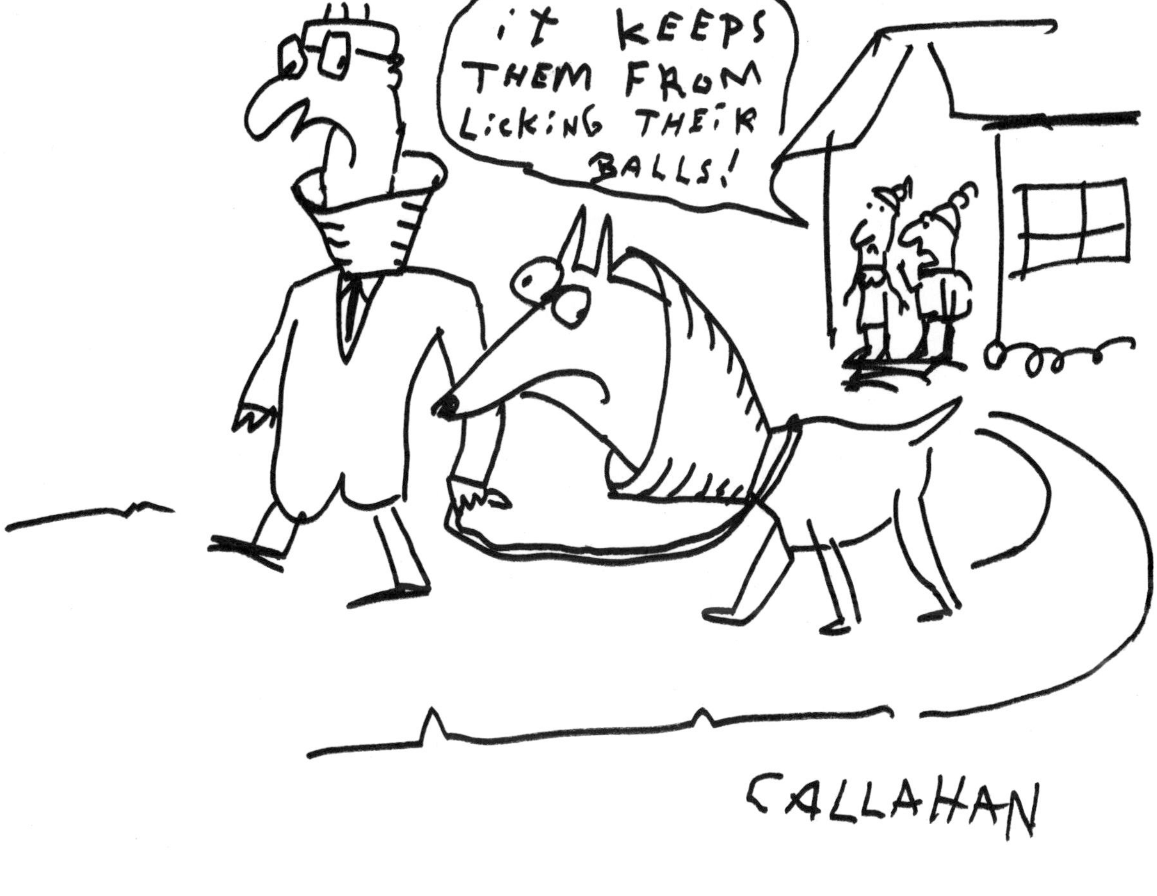
IT KEEPS THEM FROM LICKING THEIR BALLS!
CALLAHAN

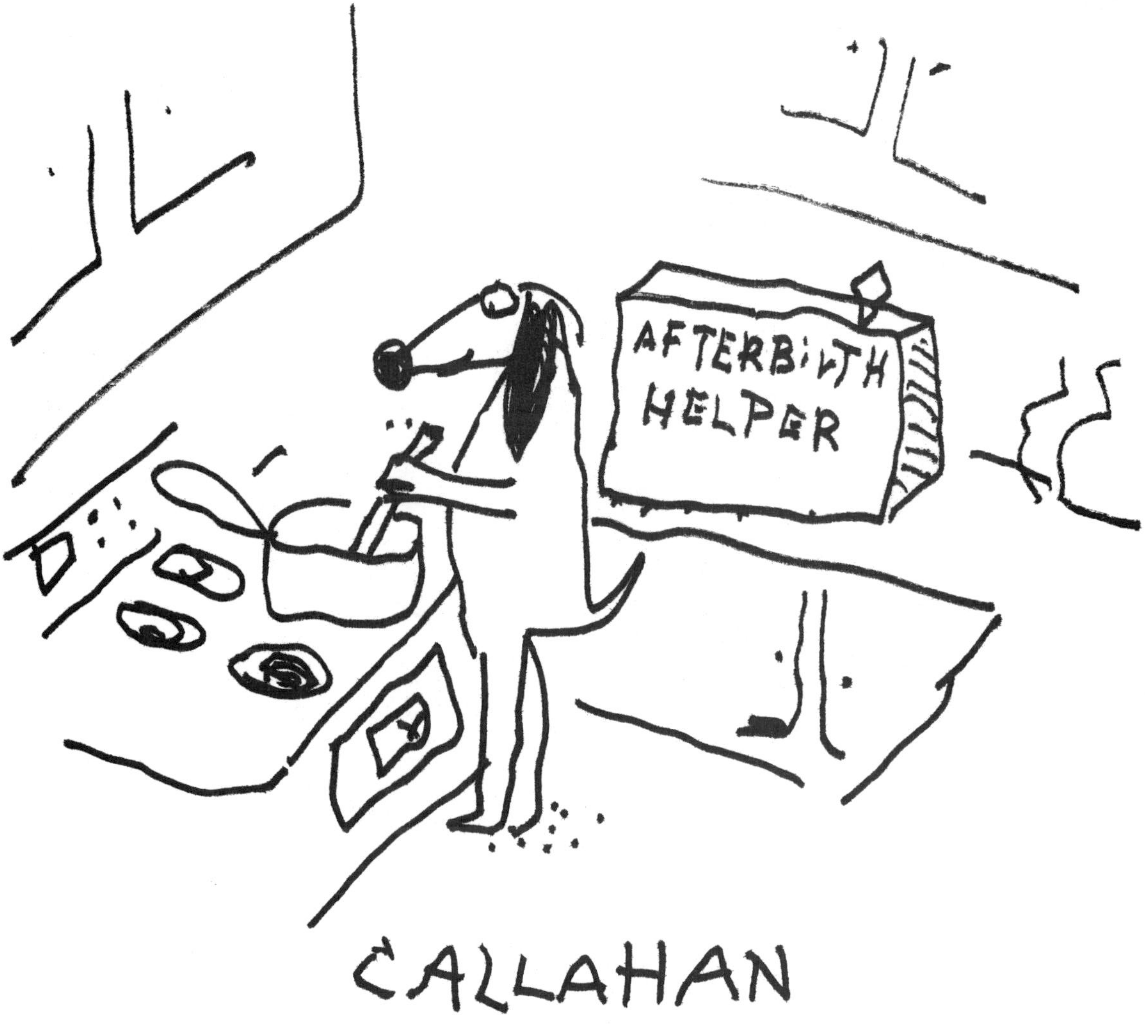
AFTERBIRTH
HELPER
CALLAHAN

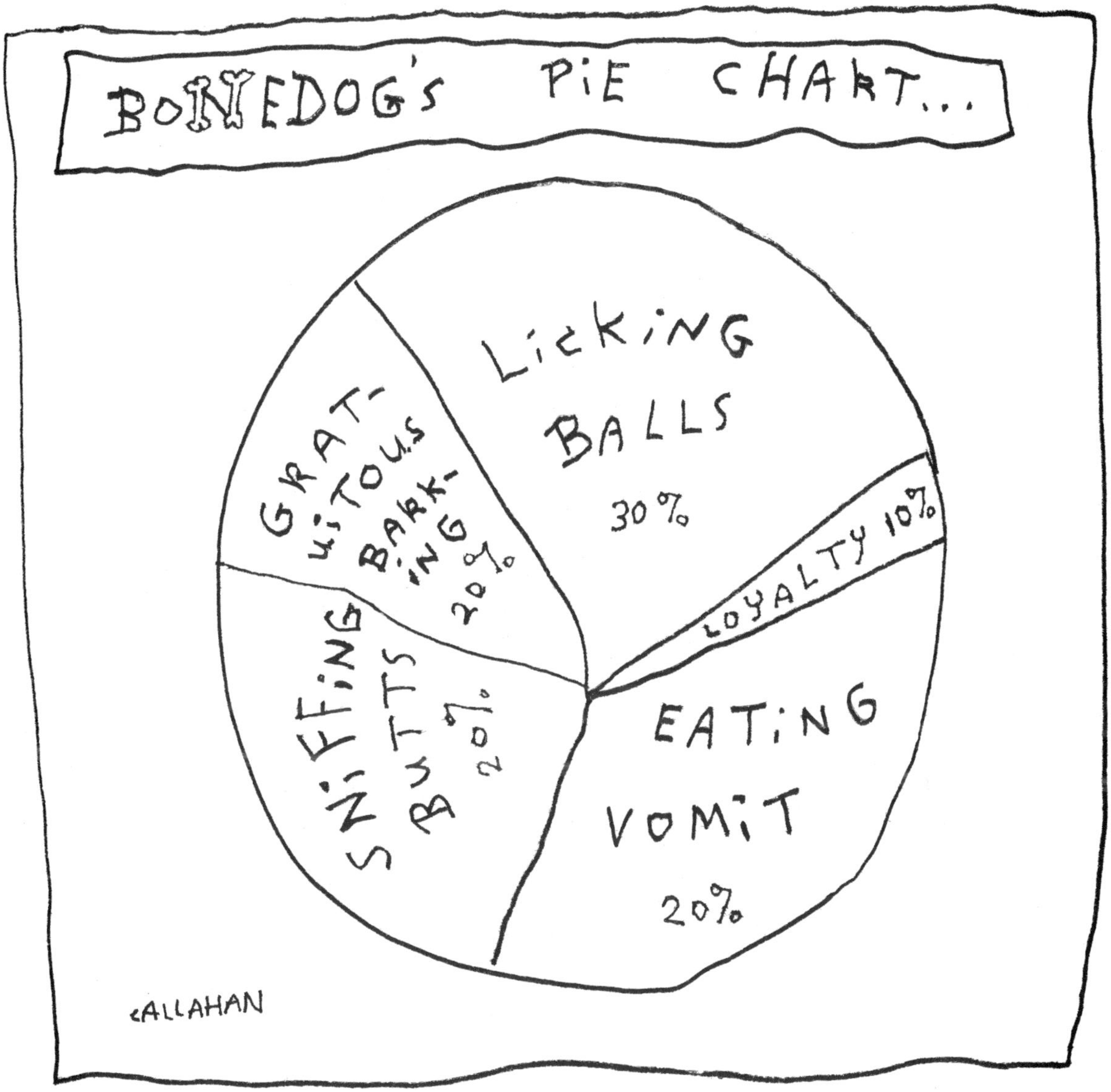
BONEDOG'S PIE CHART...
LICKING BALLS 30%
LOYALTY 10%
EATING VOMIT 20%
SNIFFING BUTTS 20%
GRAT-UITOUS BARK-ING 20%
CALLAHAN

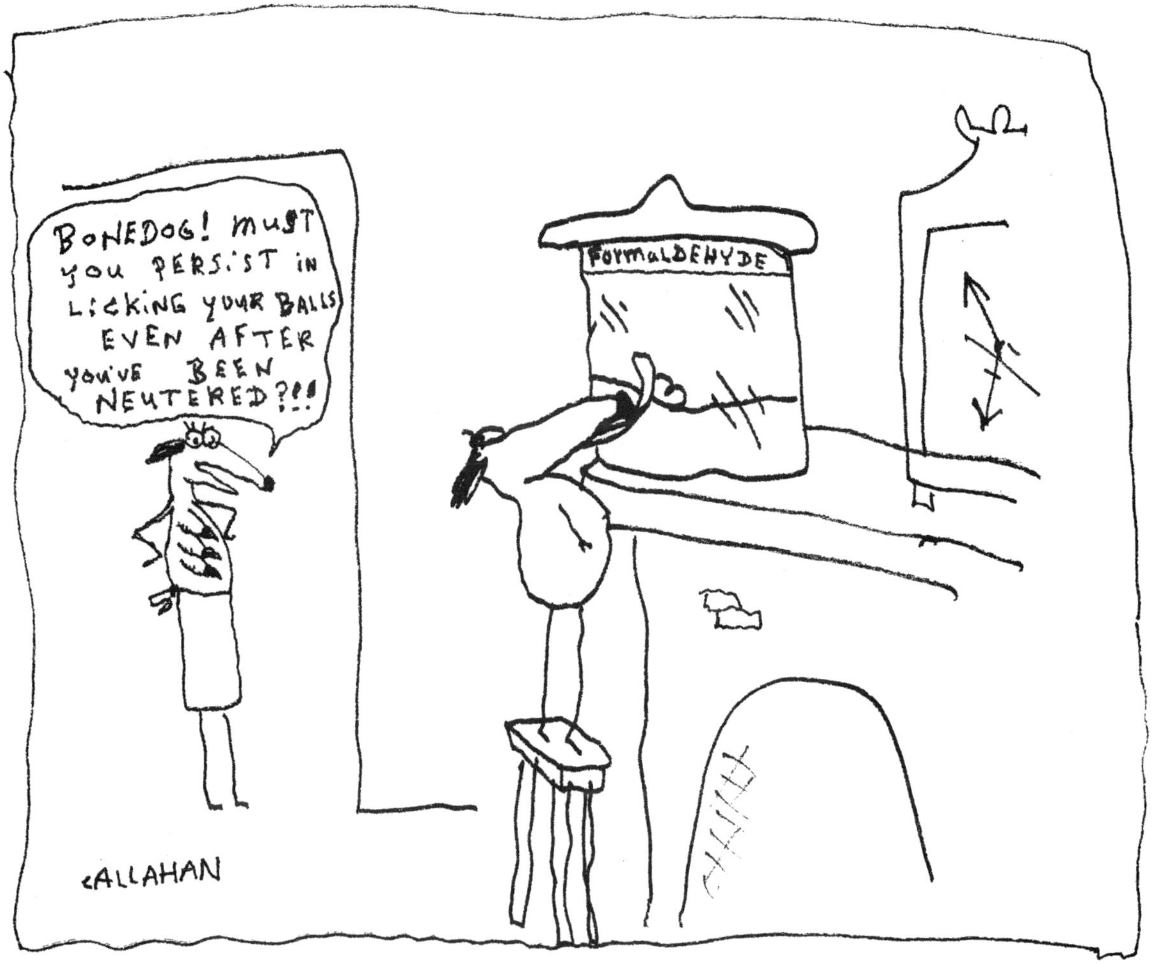
BONEDOG! MUST YOU PERSIST IN LICKING YOUR BALLS EVEN AFTER YOU'VE BEEN NEUTERED?!!
FORMALDEHYDE
CALLAHAN

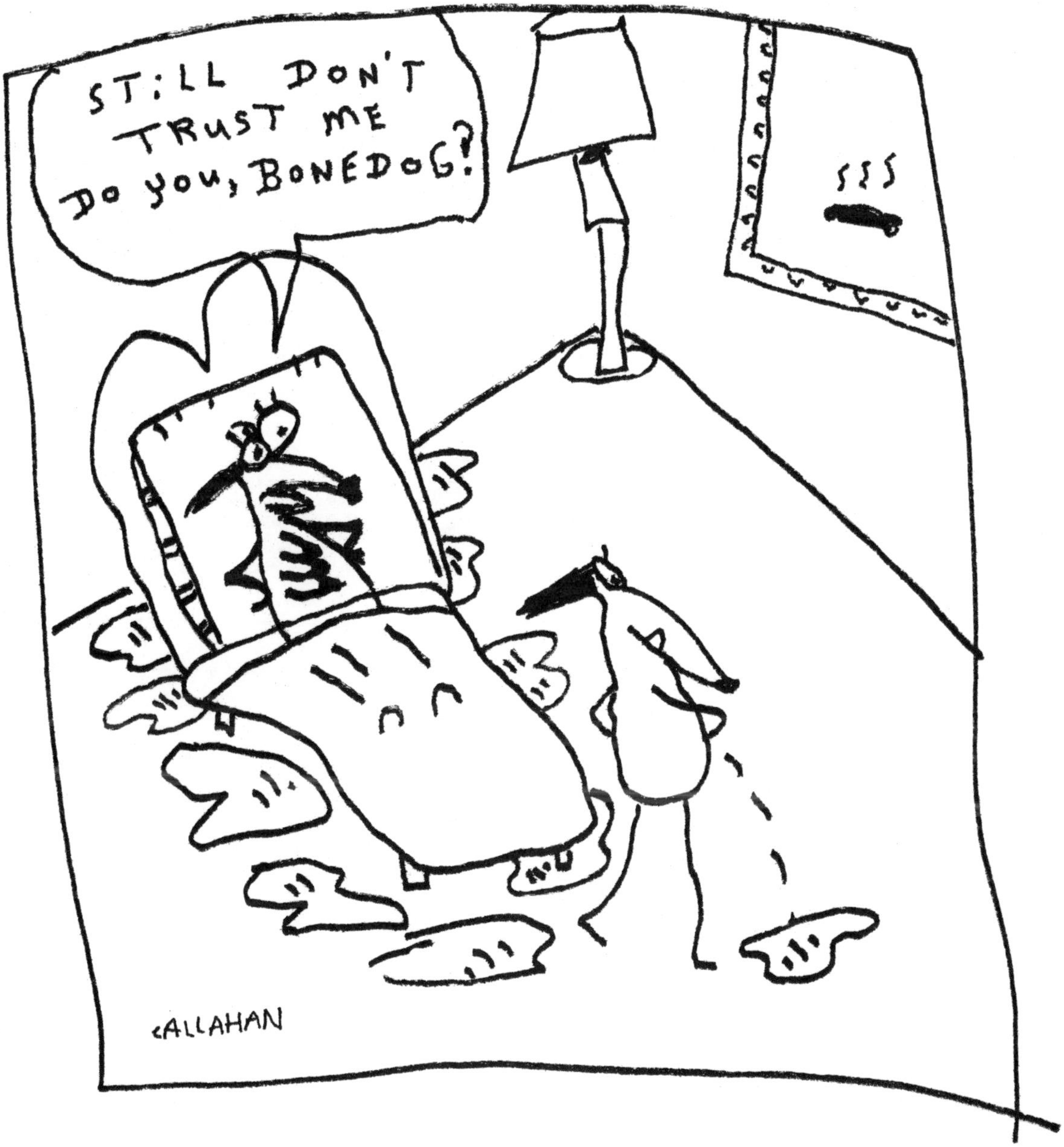
STILL DON'T TRUST ME DO YOU, BONEDOG?
CALLAHAN

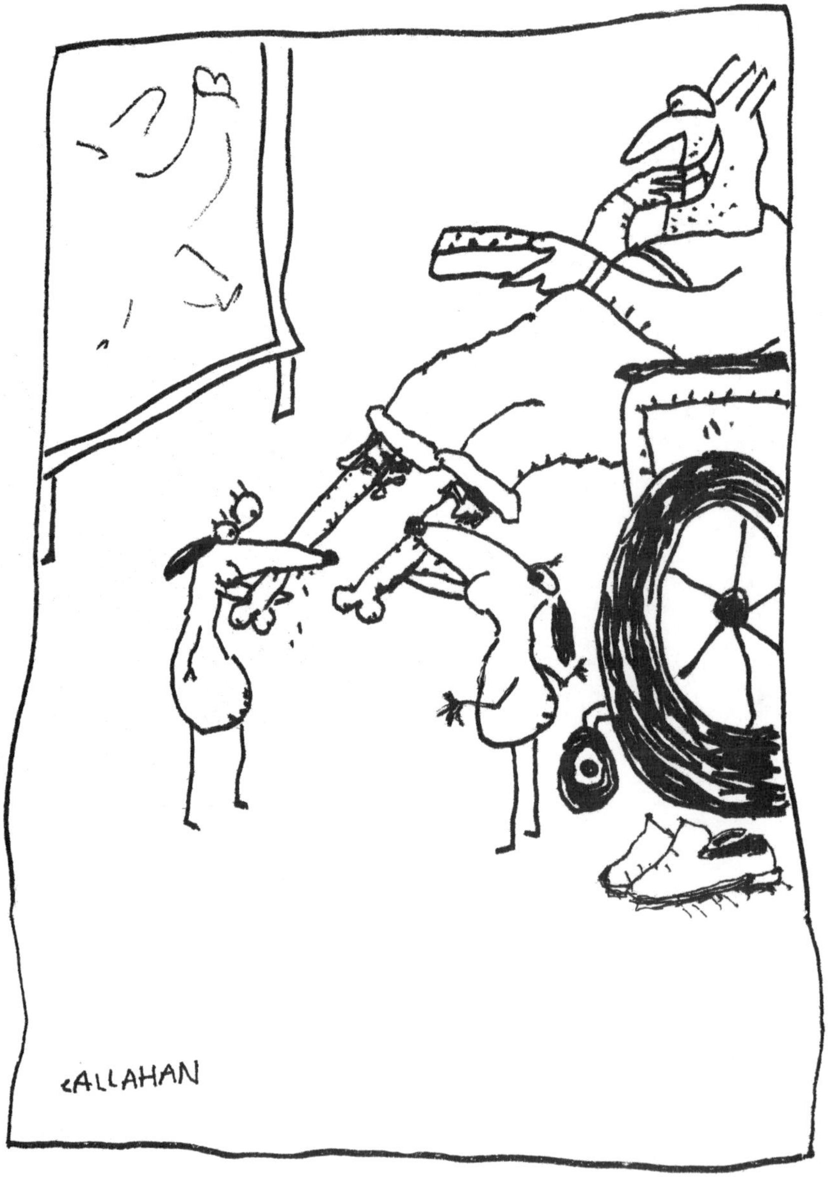
CALLAHAN

"It's one of the advantages of being Callahan's dog."

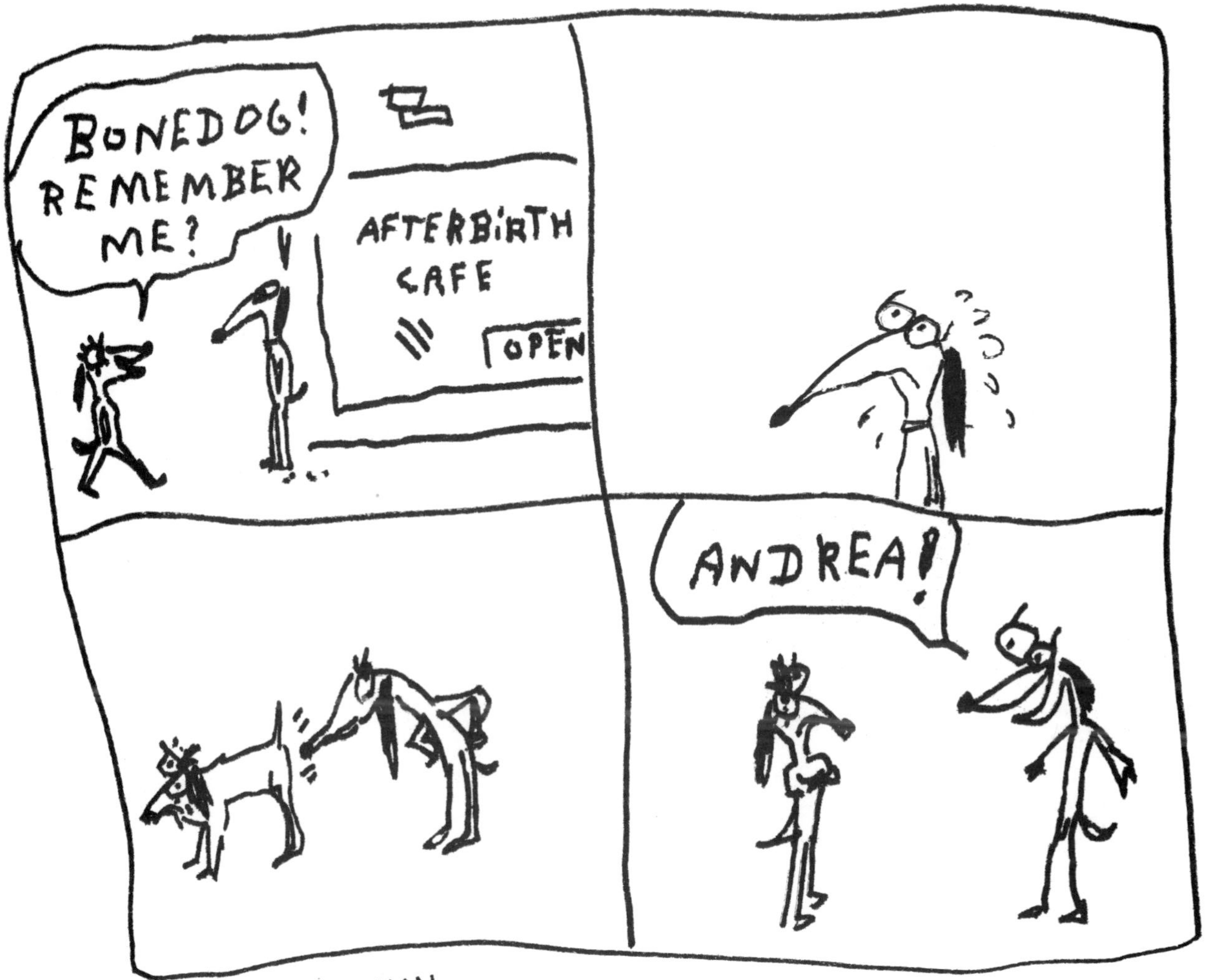
BONEDOG! REMEMBER ME?
AFTERBIRTH CAFE
OPEN
ANDREA!

CALLAHAN

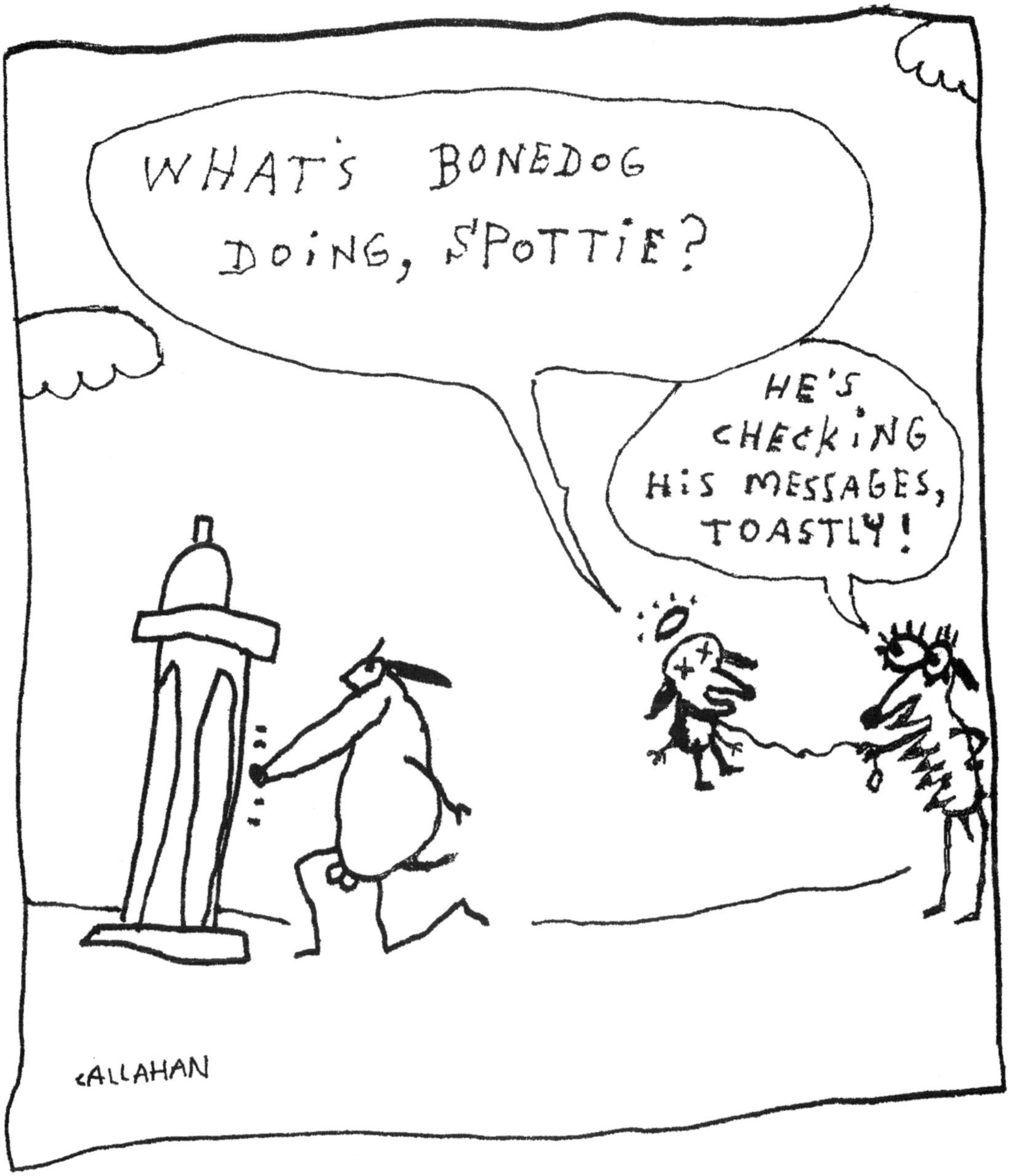
WHAT'S BONEDOG DOING, SPOTTIE?
HE'S CHECKING HIS MESSAGES, TOASTLY!
CALLAHAN

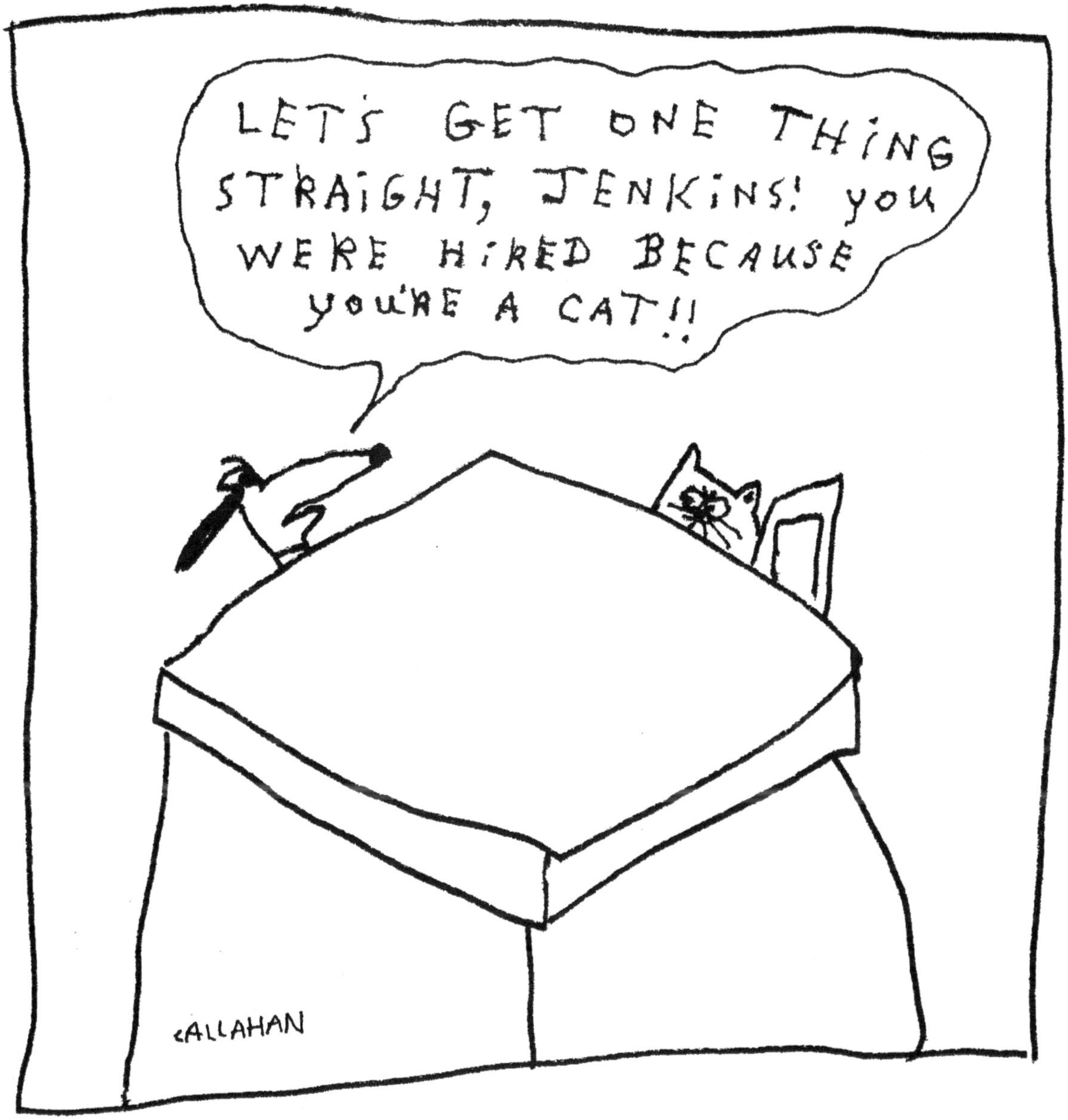
LET'S GET ONE THING STRAIGHT, JENKINS! YOU WERE HIRED BECAUSE YOU'RE A CAT!!
CALLAHAN

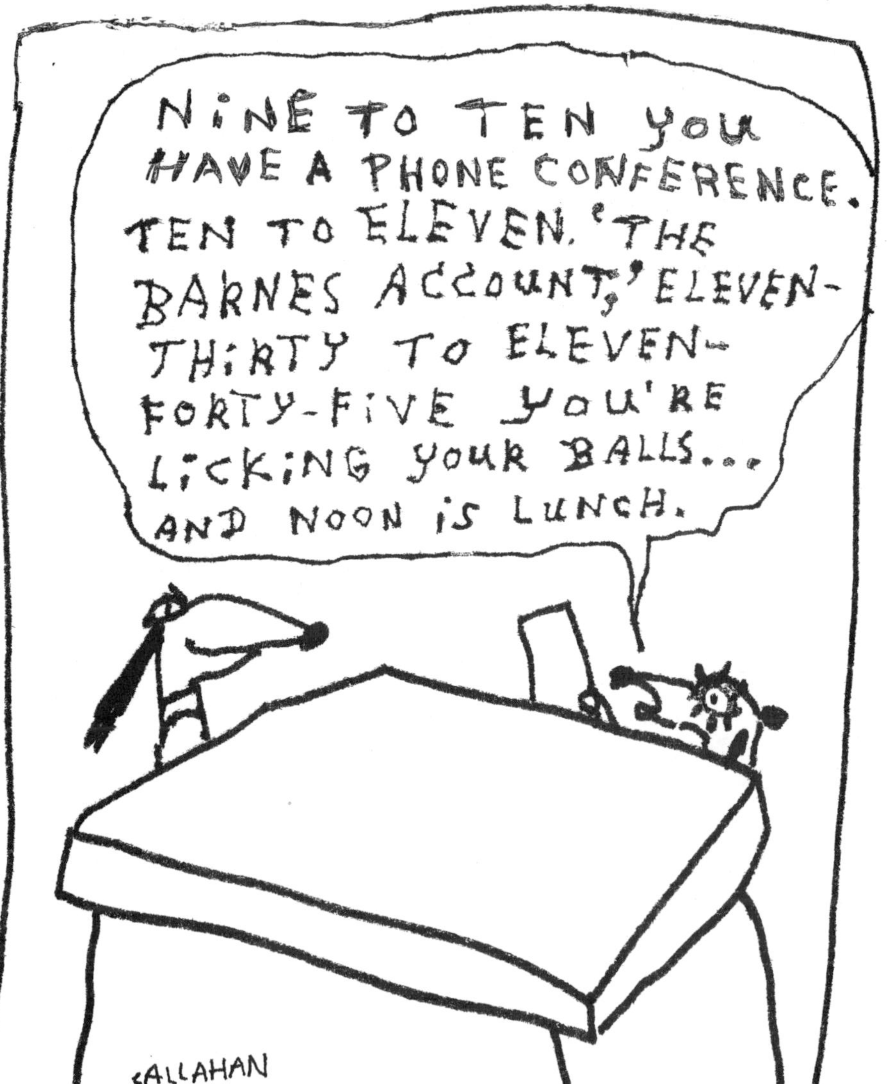
NINE TO TEN YOU HAVE A PHONE CONFERENCE. TEN TO ELEVEN, 'THE BARNES ACCOUNT,' ELEVEN-THIRTY TO ELEVEN-FORTY-FIVE YOU'RE LICKING YOUR BALLS... AND NOON IS LUNCH.
CALLAHAN

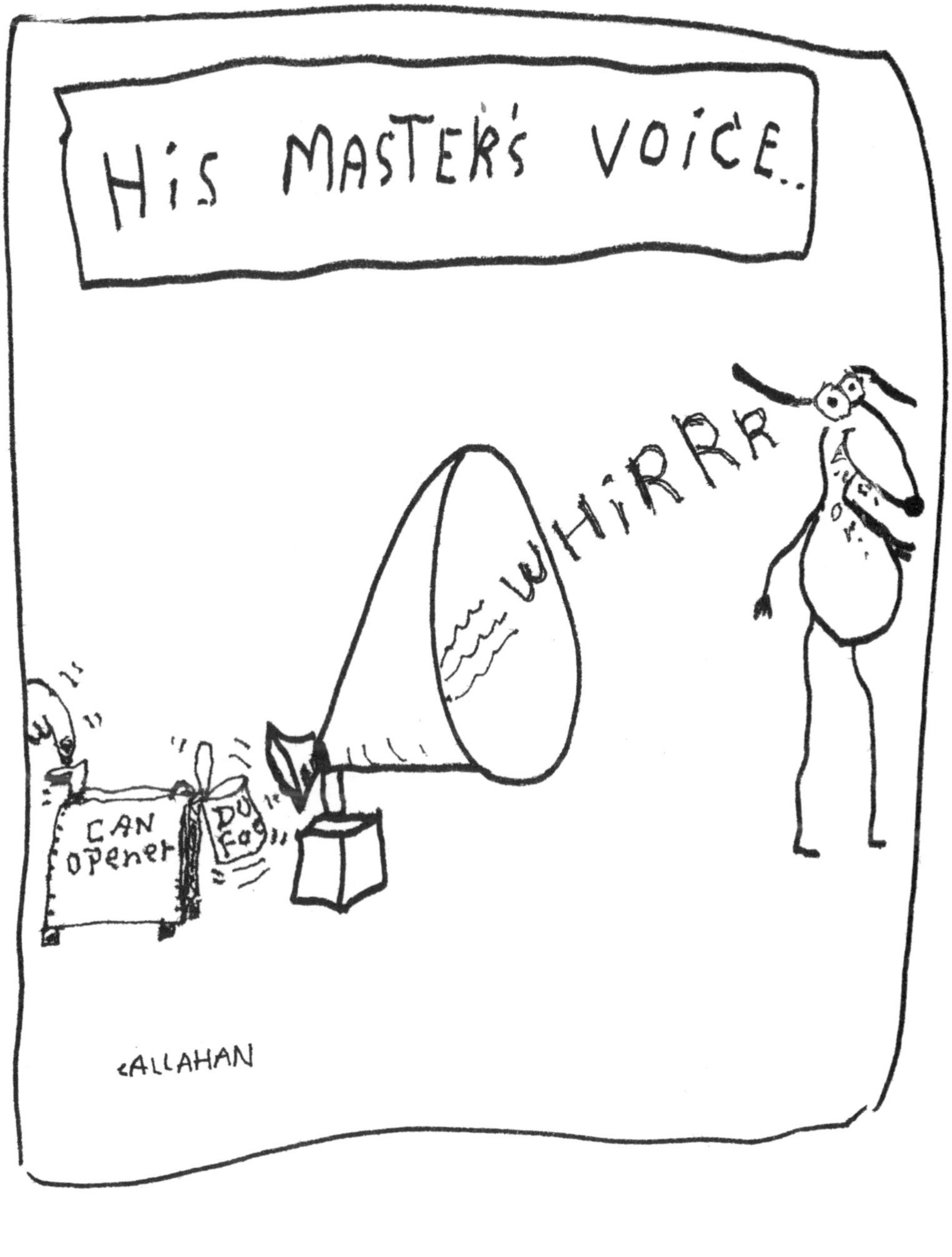
HIS MASTER'S VOICE..
WHIRRR
CAN opener
CALLAHAN

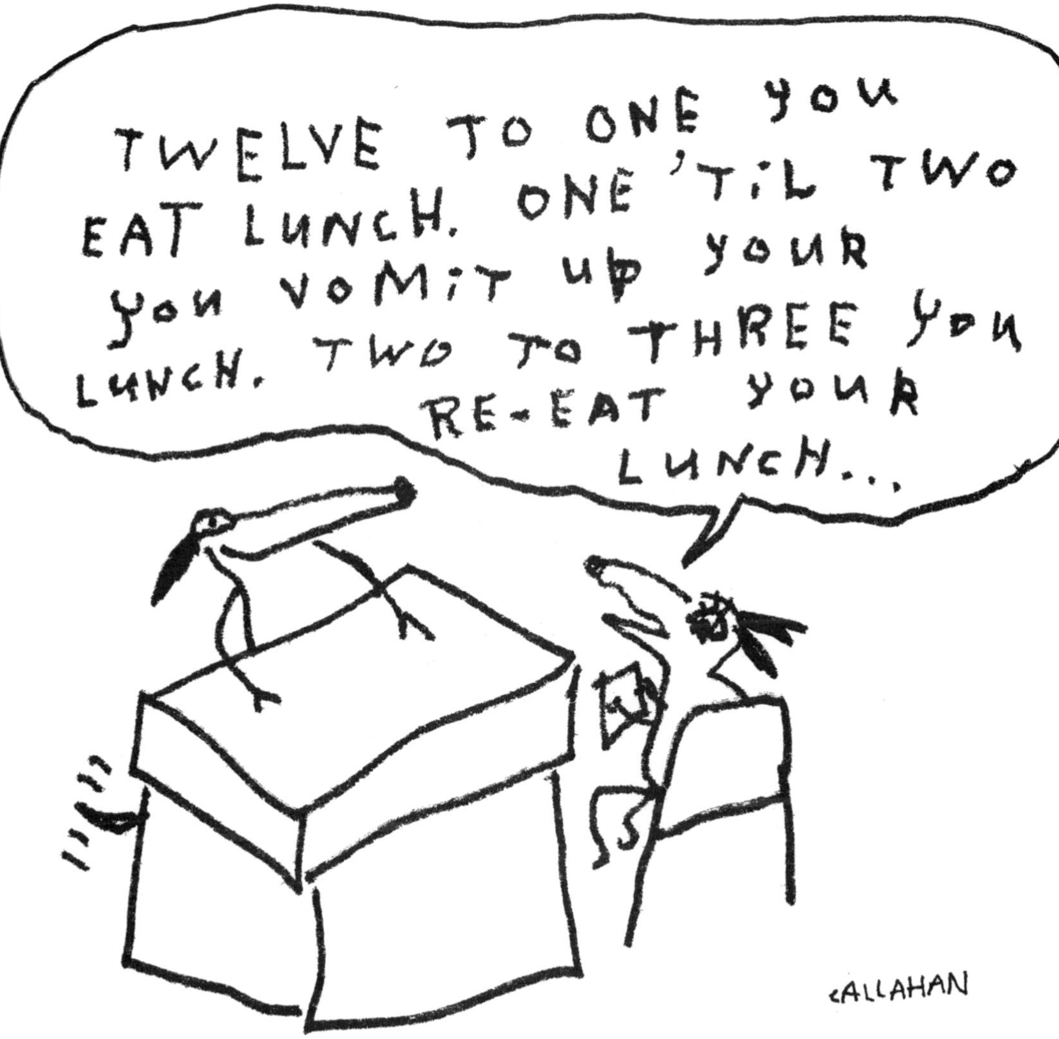
TWELVE TO ONE YOU EAT LUNCH. ONE 'TIL TWO YOU VOMIT UP YOUR LUNCH. TWO TO THREE YOU RE-EAT YOUR LUNCH...
CALLAHAN

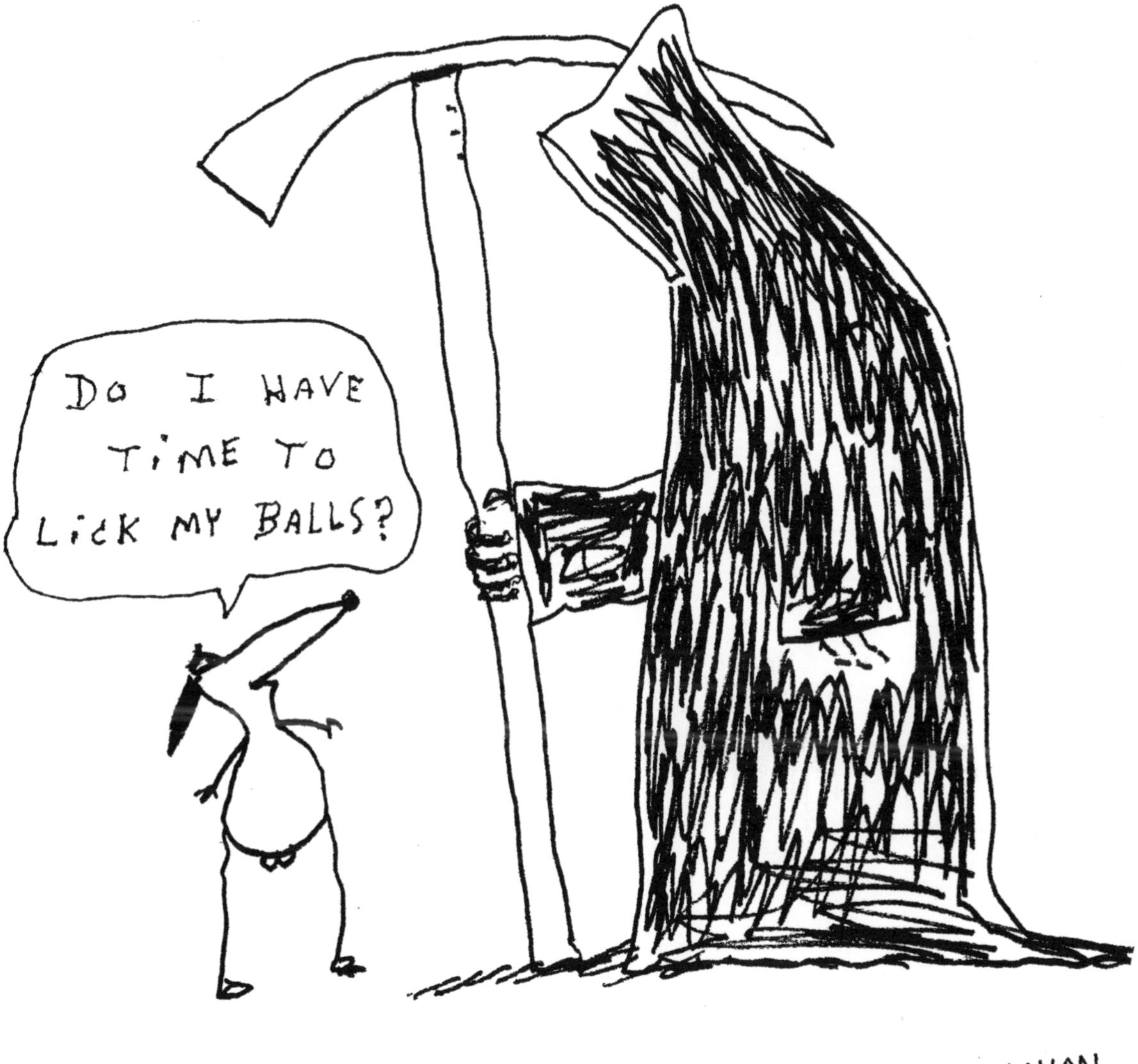
DO I HAVE TIME TO LICK MY BALLS?
CALLAHAN

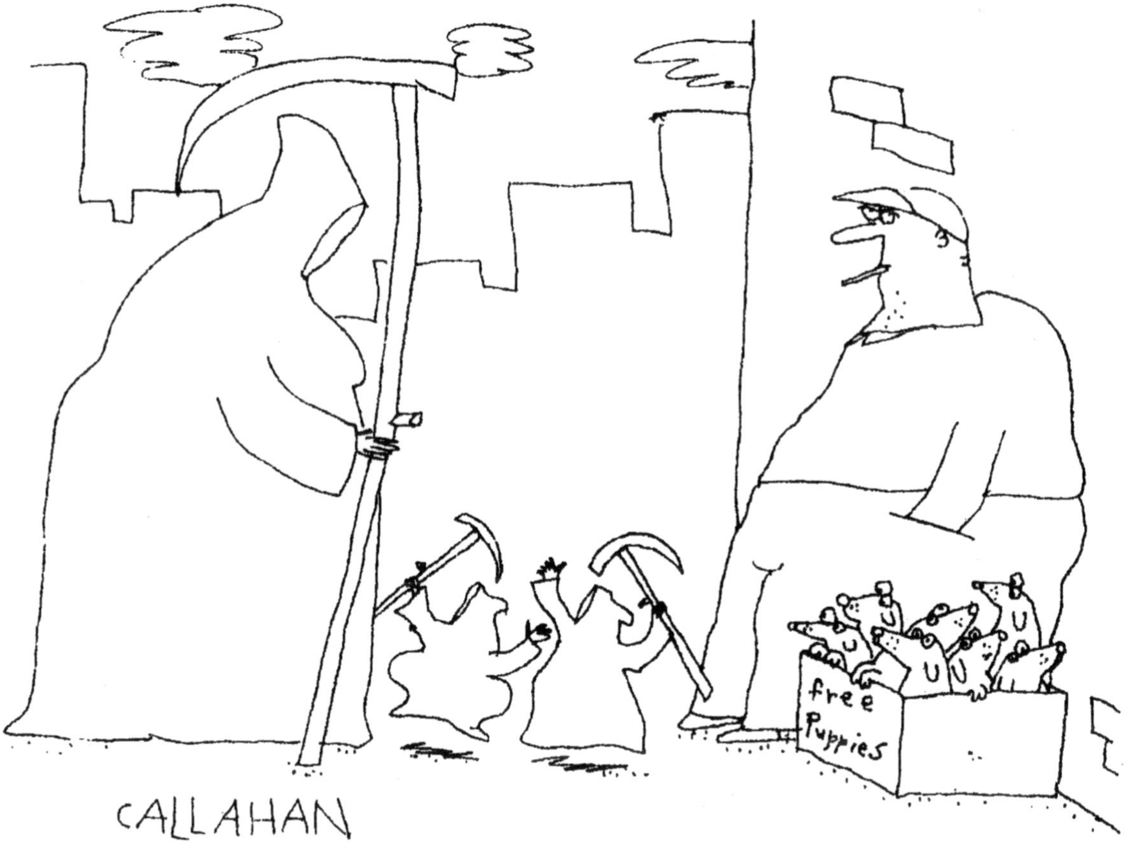
CALLAHAN
free Puppies

"Mommy! Mommy! Can we kill the puppies?!!"

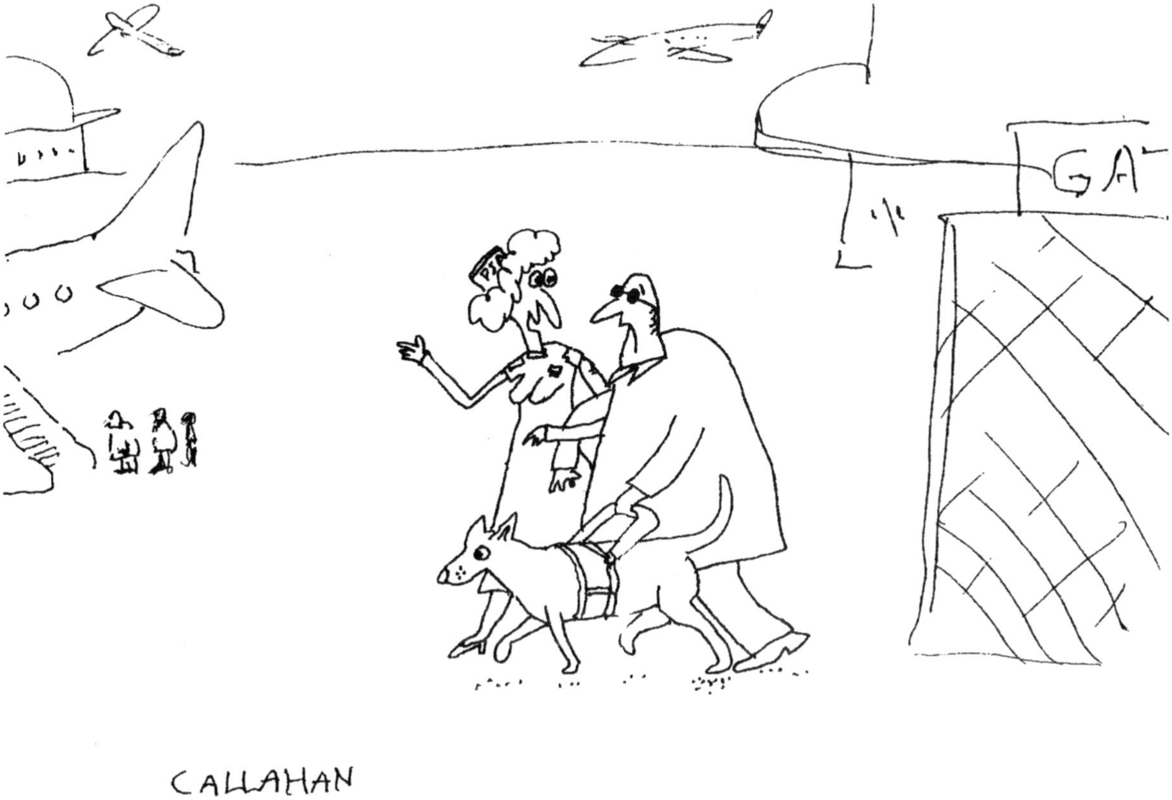
GA
CALLAHAN

"...and we've arranged a window seat for your dog so you can enjoy the view!!"

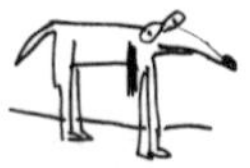

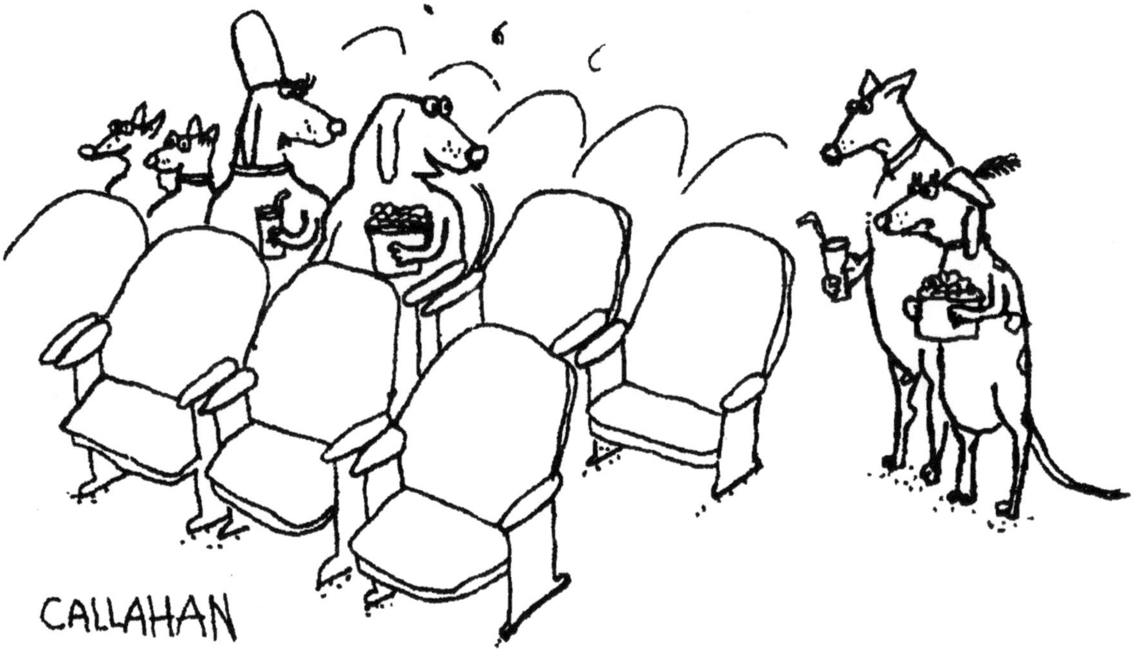
CALLAHAN

"Excuse me, but I think those seats have already been pissed around."

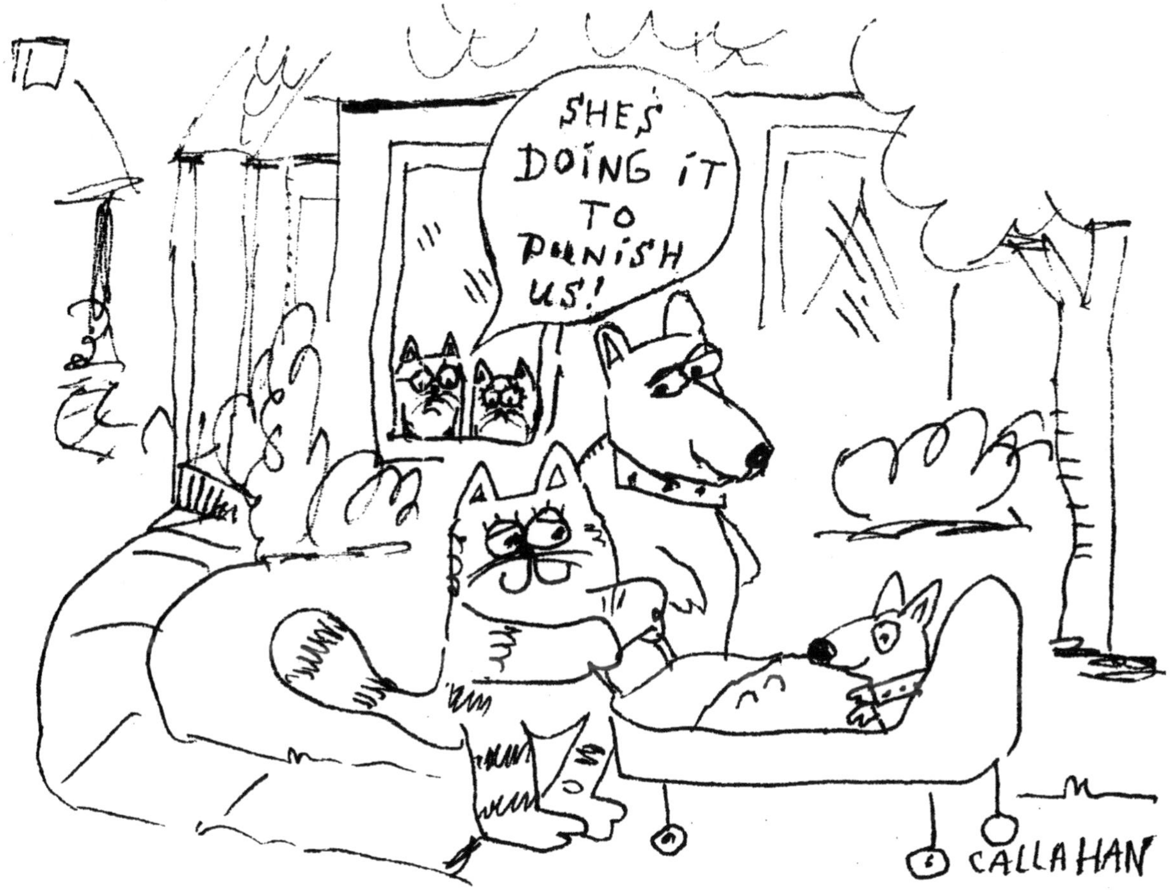
SHE'S DOING IT TO PUNISH US!
CALLAHAN

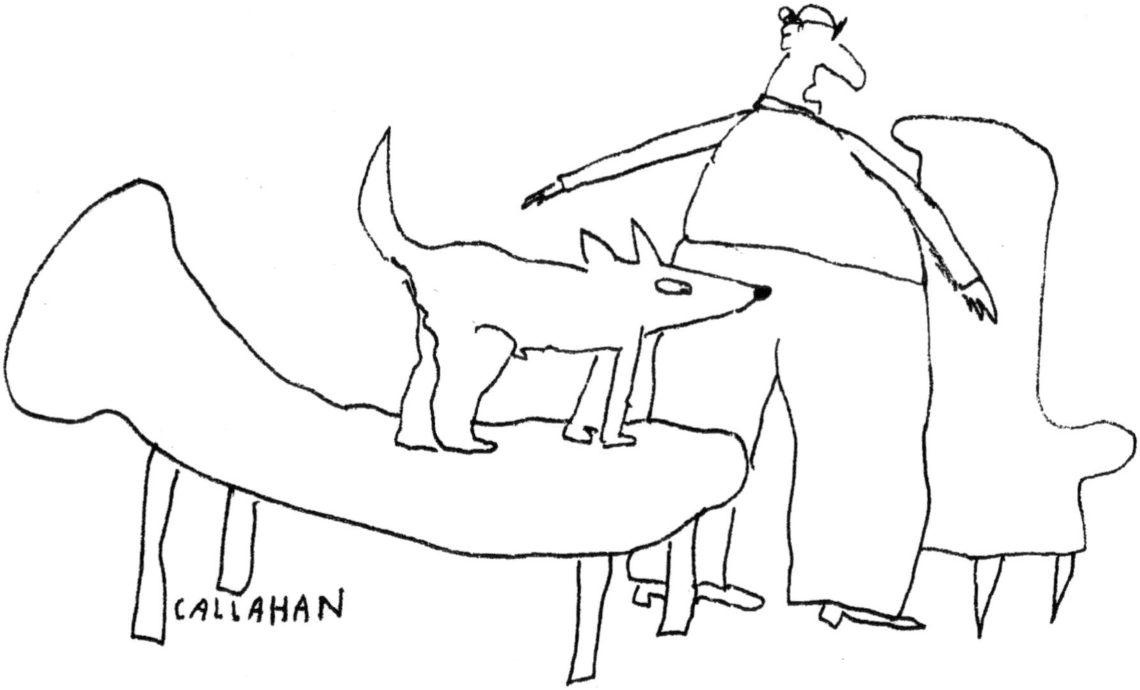
CALLAHAN

"Take your time...
It's important to choose the right therapist."

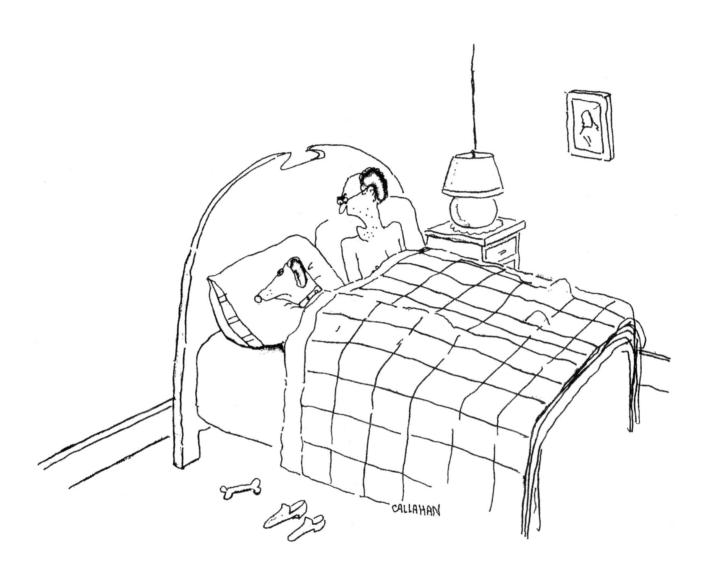

"That's right, forget about my feelings!
Just roll over and play dead!"

HEAL!
CALLAHAN

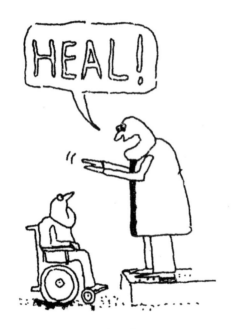

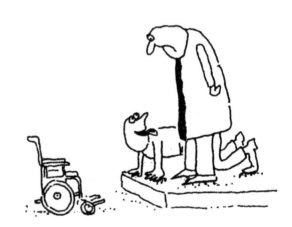

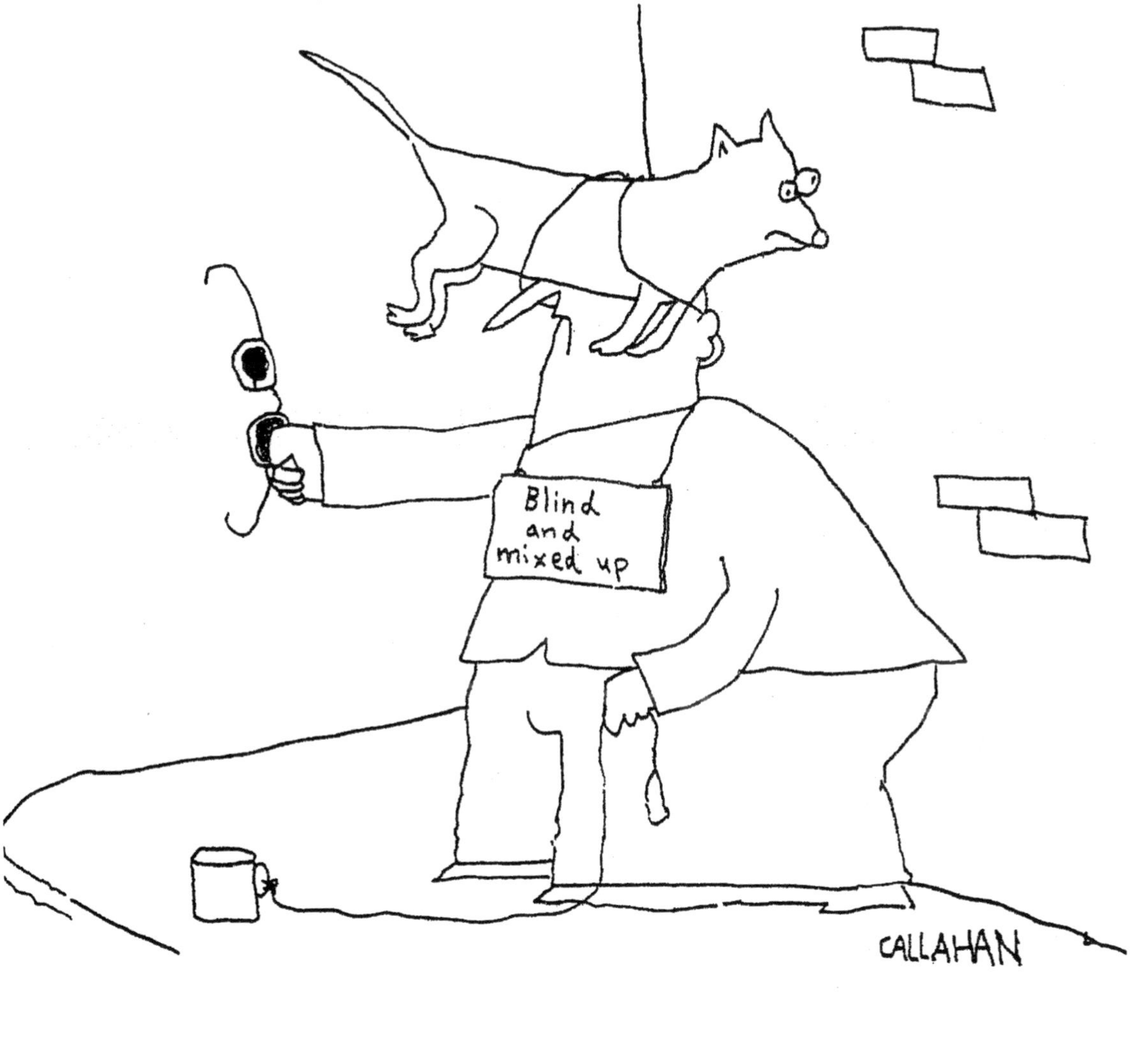
Blind
and
mixed up
CALLAHAN

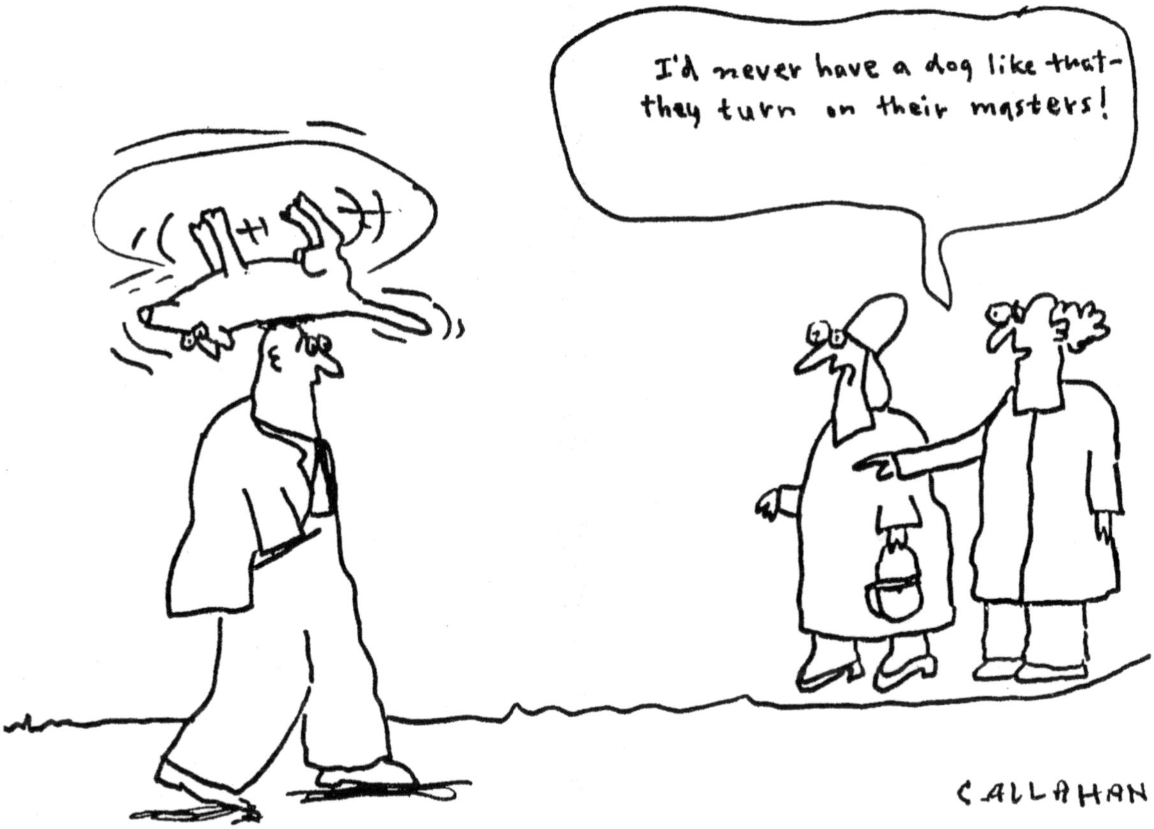
I'd never have a dog like that-
they turn on their masters!
CALLAHAN

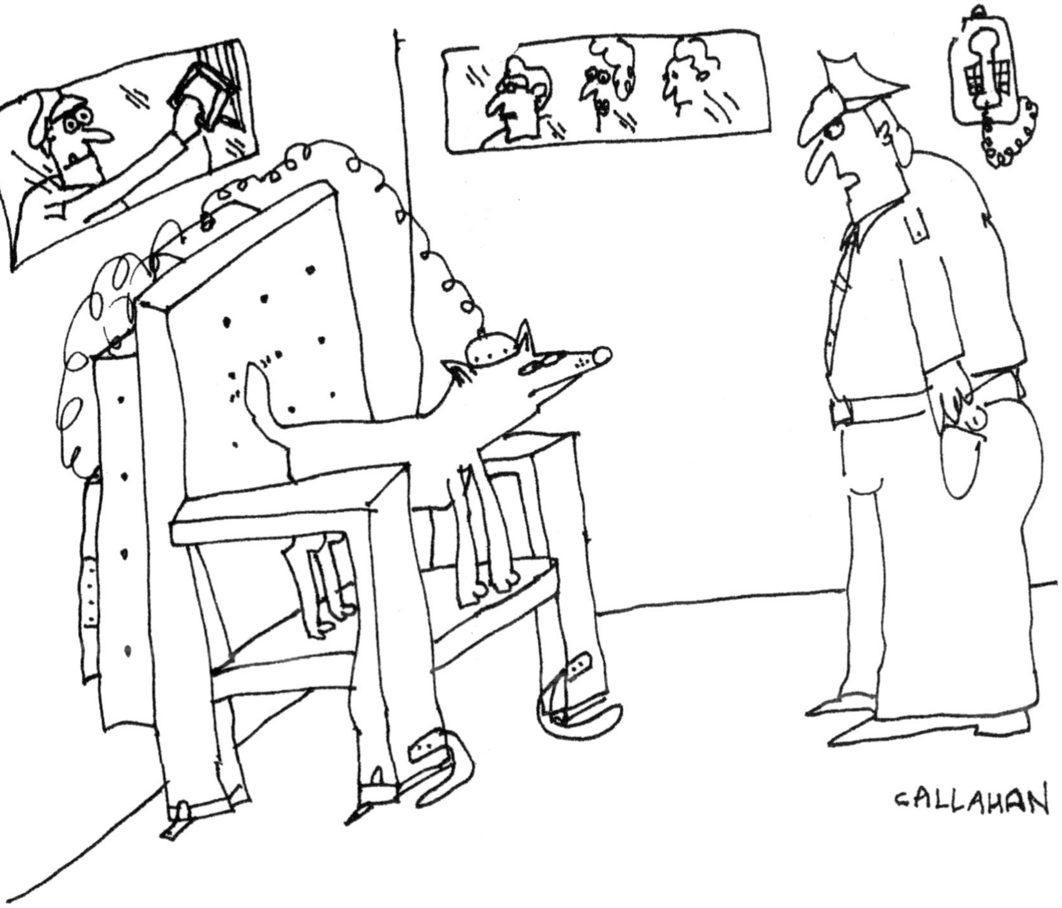
CALLAHAN

"Sit!...Sit!...Sit!...Sit!...Sit!...Sit!...Sit!..."

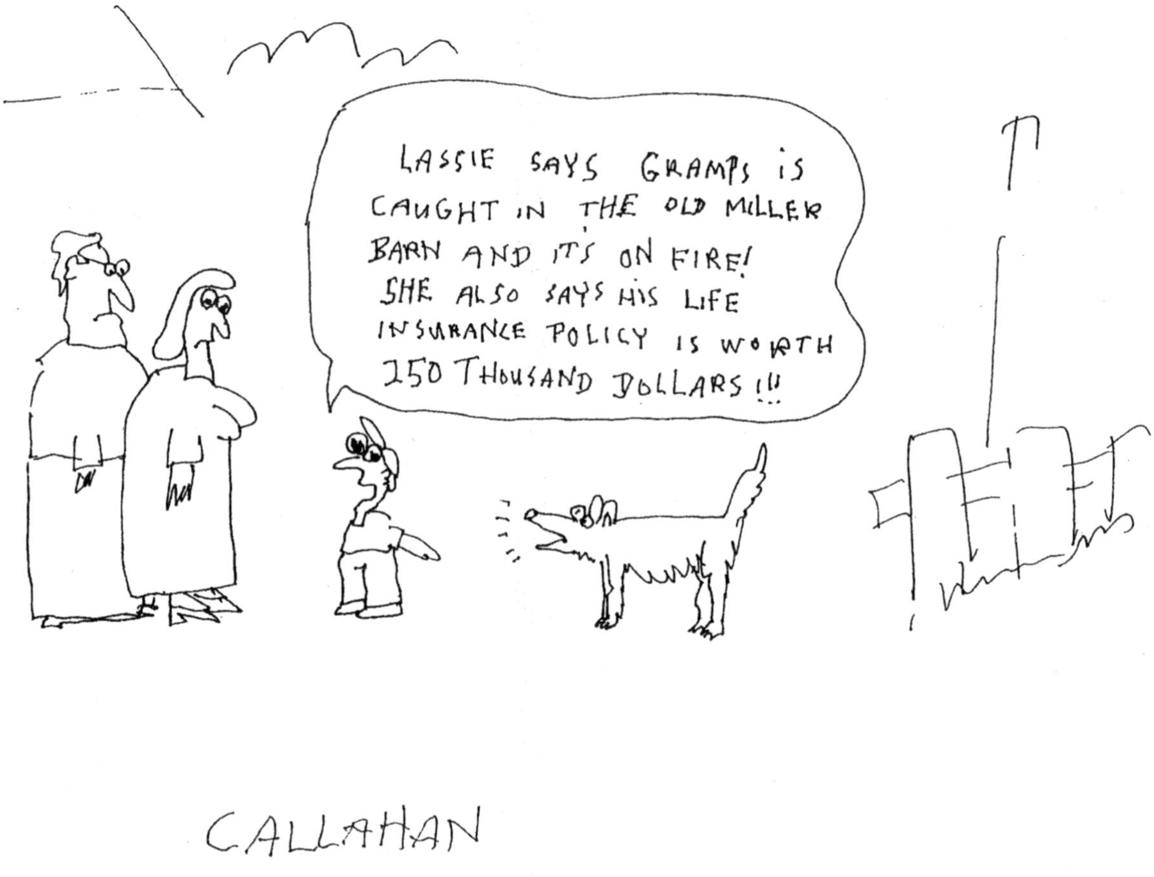
LASSIE SAYS GRAMPS IS CAUGHT IN THE OLD MILLER BARN AND IT'S ON FIRE! SHE ALSO SAYS HIS LIFE INSURANCE POLICY IS WORTH 250 THOUSAND DOLLARS!!!
CALLAHAN

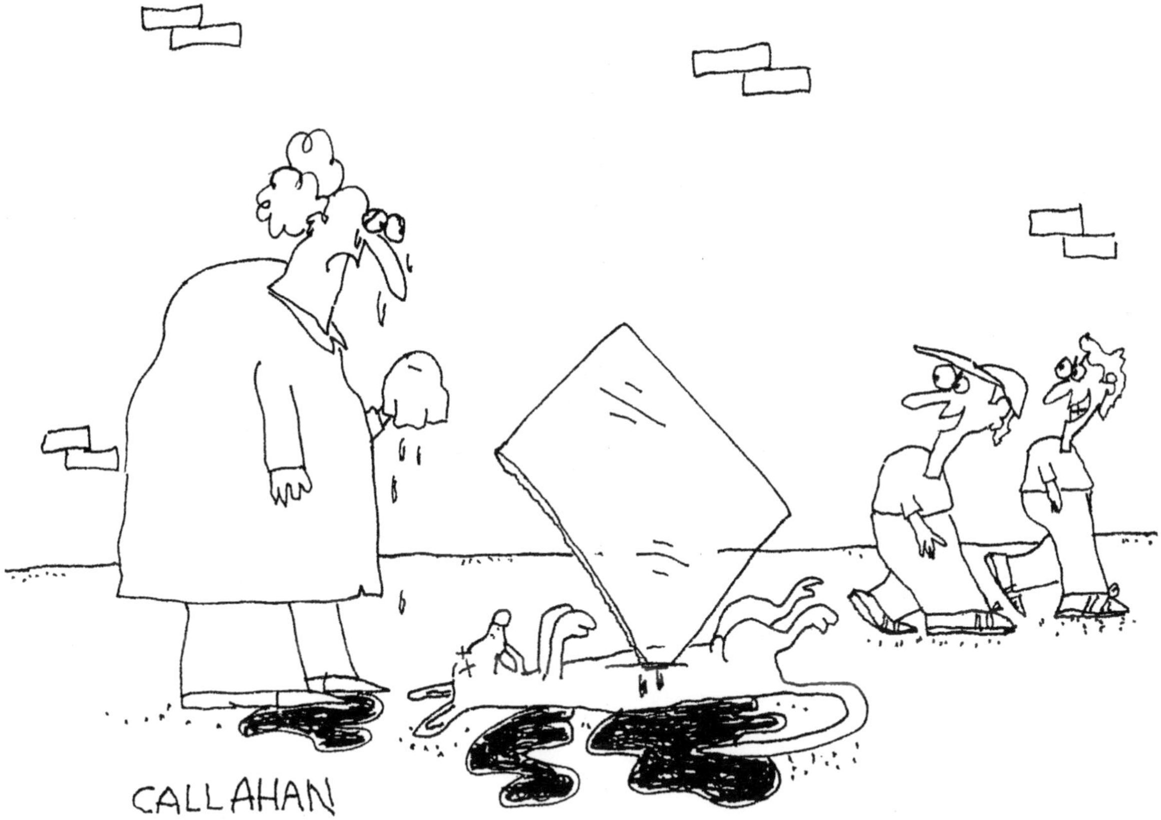
CALLAHAN

"How much is that window in the doggie?"

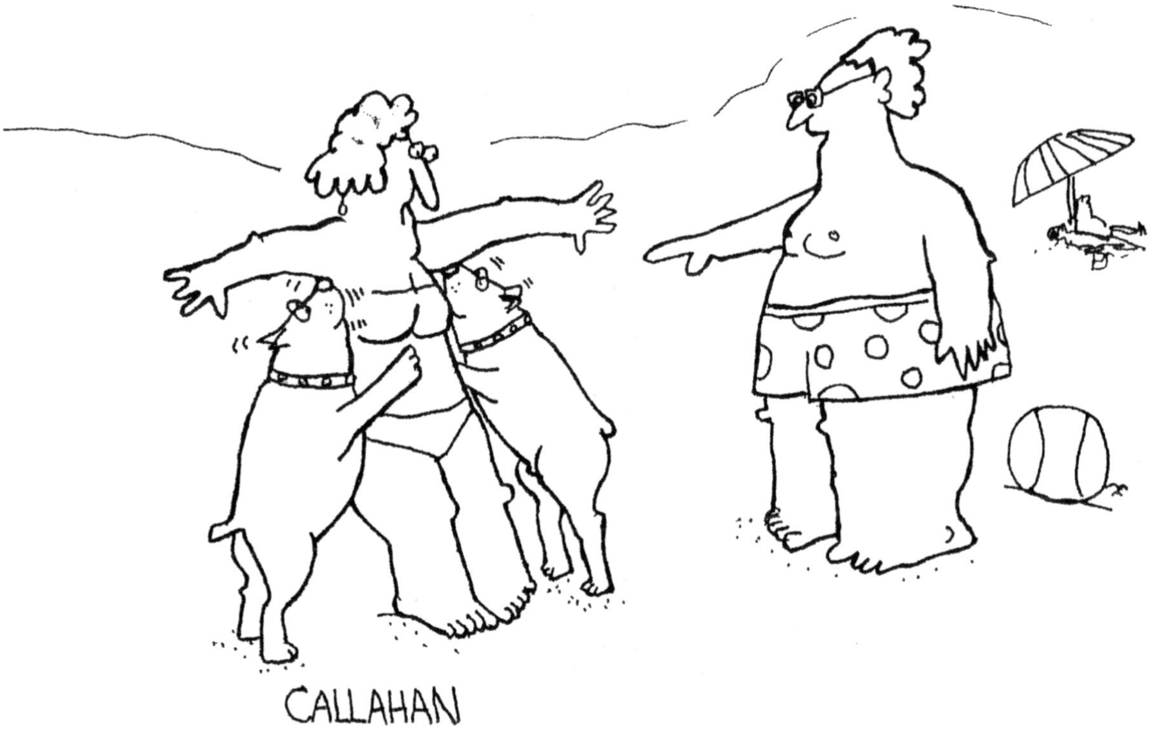
CALLAHAN

"So that's why they call them pit bulls!"

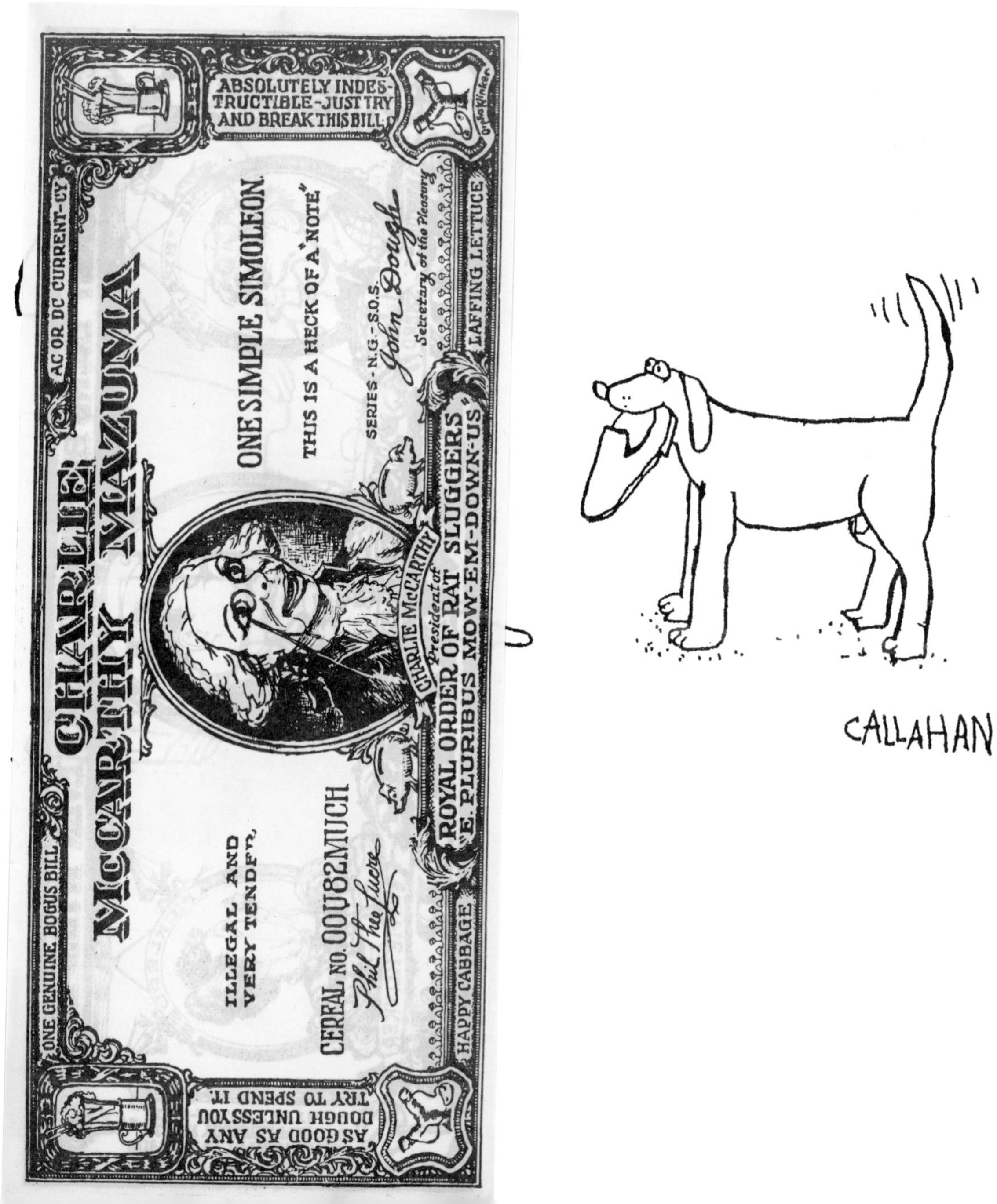
ONE GENUINE BOGUS BILL
AC OR DC CURRENT-CY
CHARLIE McCARTHY MAZUMA
ABSOLUTELY INDESTRUCTIBLE - JUST TRY AND BREAK THIS BILL
ONE SIMPLE SIMOLEON
THIS IS A HECK OF A "NOTE"
SERIES - N.G. - S.O.S.
John Dough
Secretary of the Pleasury
ILLEGAL AND VERY TENDER
CEREAL NO. 00U82MUCH
Phil Thee Lucre
CHARLIE McCARTHY
President of
ROYAL ORDER OF RAT SLUGGERS
E. PLURIBUS MOW-EM-DOWN-US
HAPPY CABBAGE
LAFFING LETTUCE
AS GOOD AS ANY DOUGH UNLESS YOU TRY TO SPEND IT.
CALLAHAN

CALLAHAN

"It seemed like the best breed for a thalidomide baby."

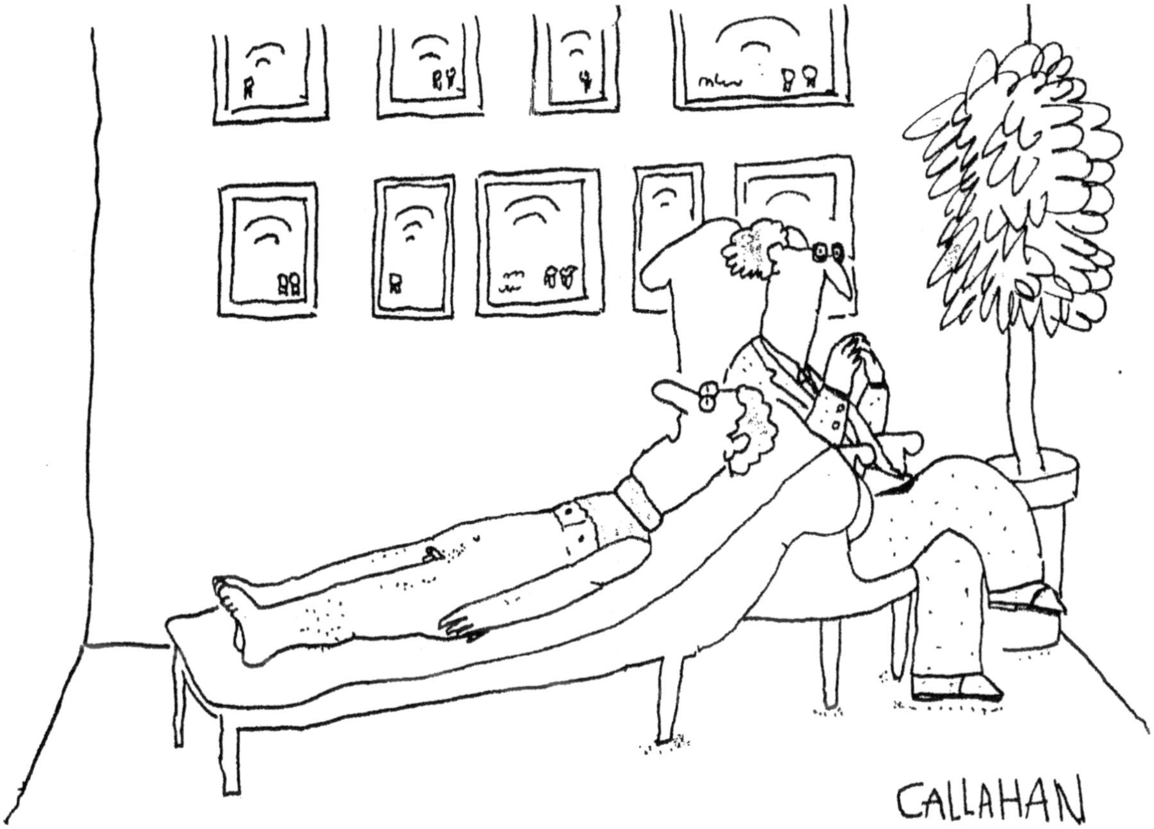
CALLAHAN

“I’ve been wearing my dog’s clothes again, Doctor.”

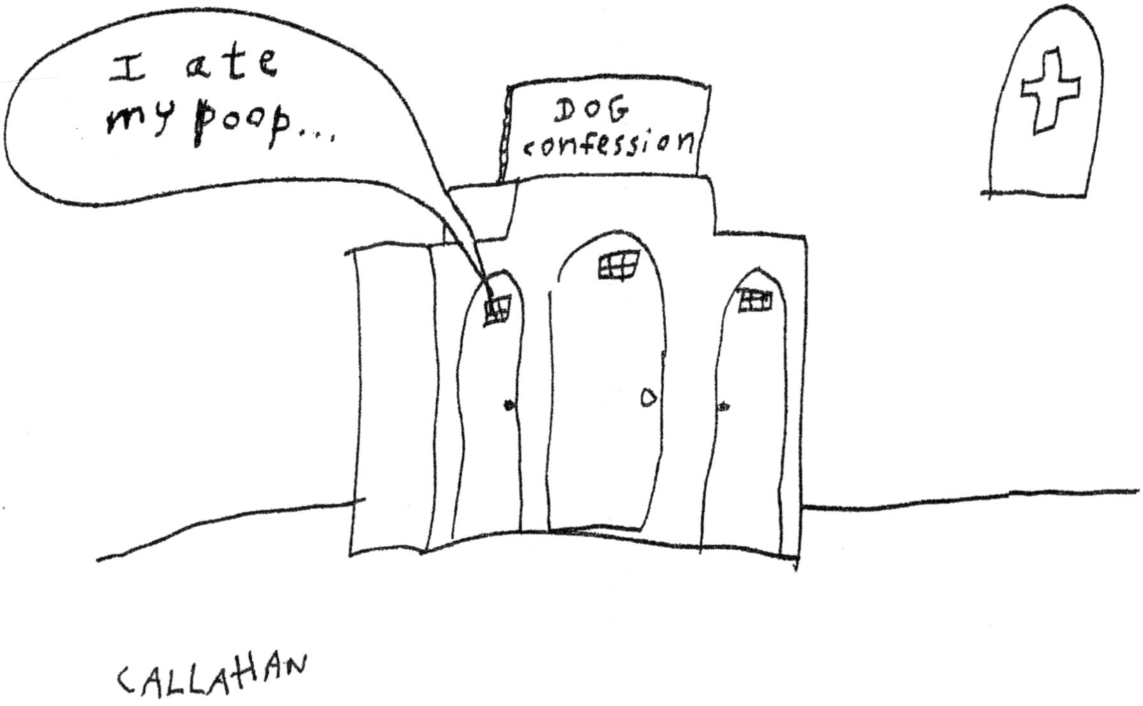
I ate my poop...
DOG confession
CALLAHAN

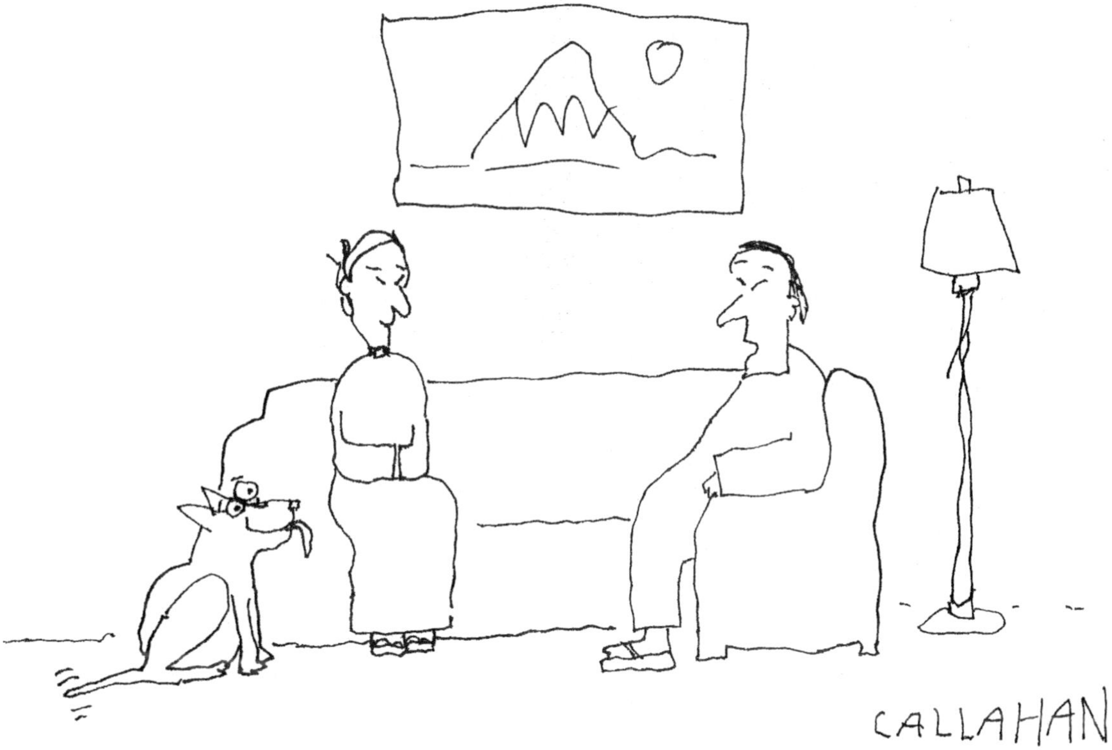
CALLAHAN

"Let's wok the dog."

in
out
in
out
in
out
in
CALLAHAH

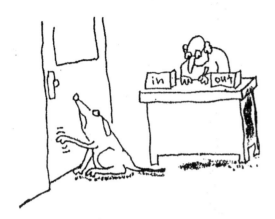

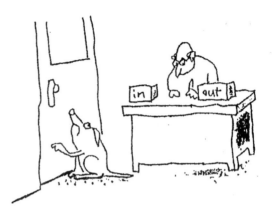

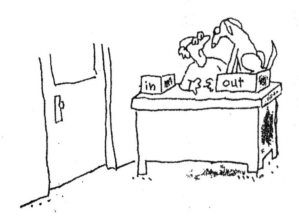

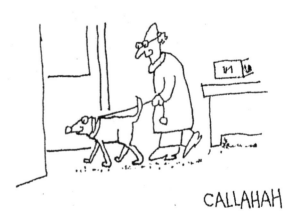

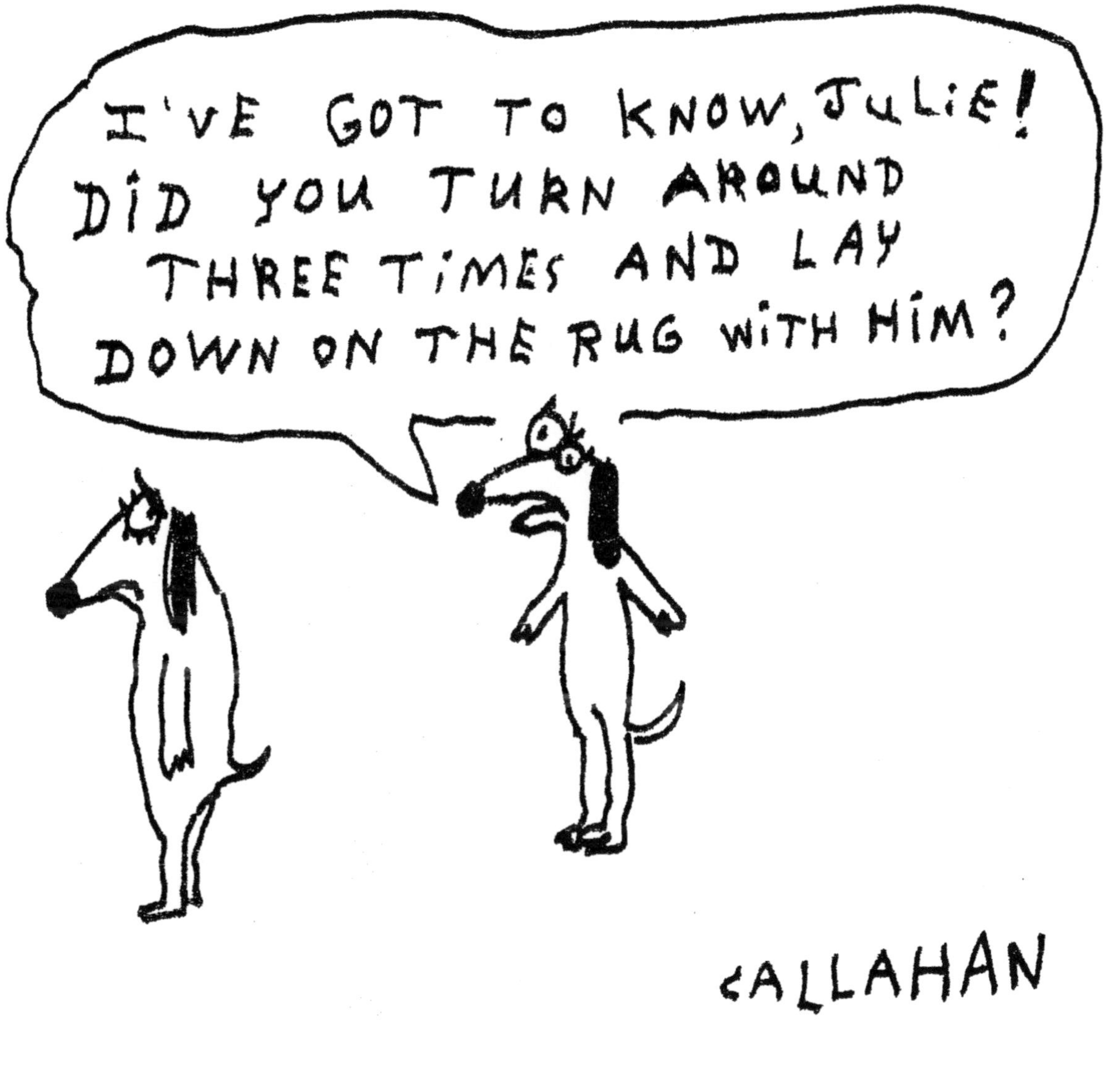
I'VE GOT TO KNOW, JULIE! DID YOU TURN AROUND THREE TIMES AND LAY DOWN ON THE RUG WITH HIM?
CALLAHAN

CALLAHAN

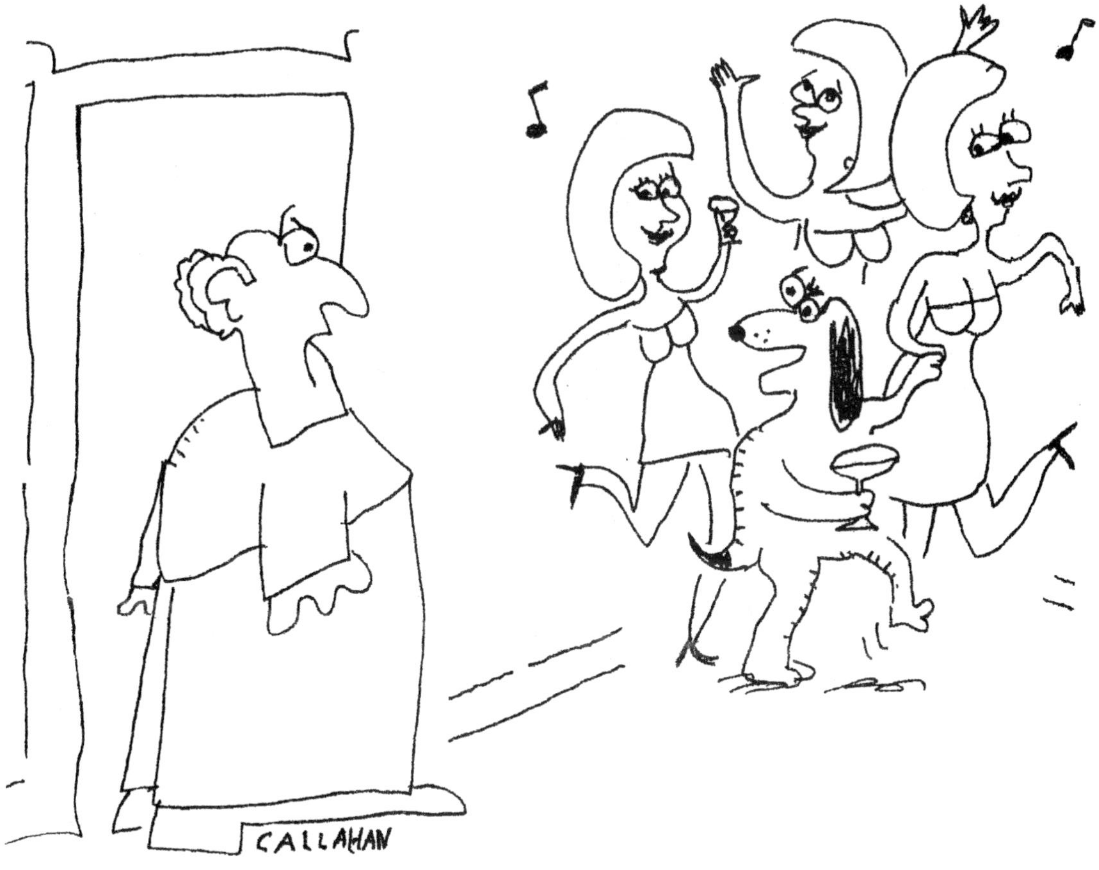
CALLAHAN

"Hey! When that leash comes off I'm on MY TIME!!"

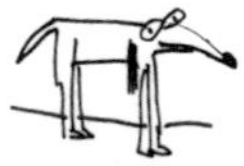

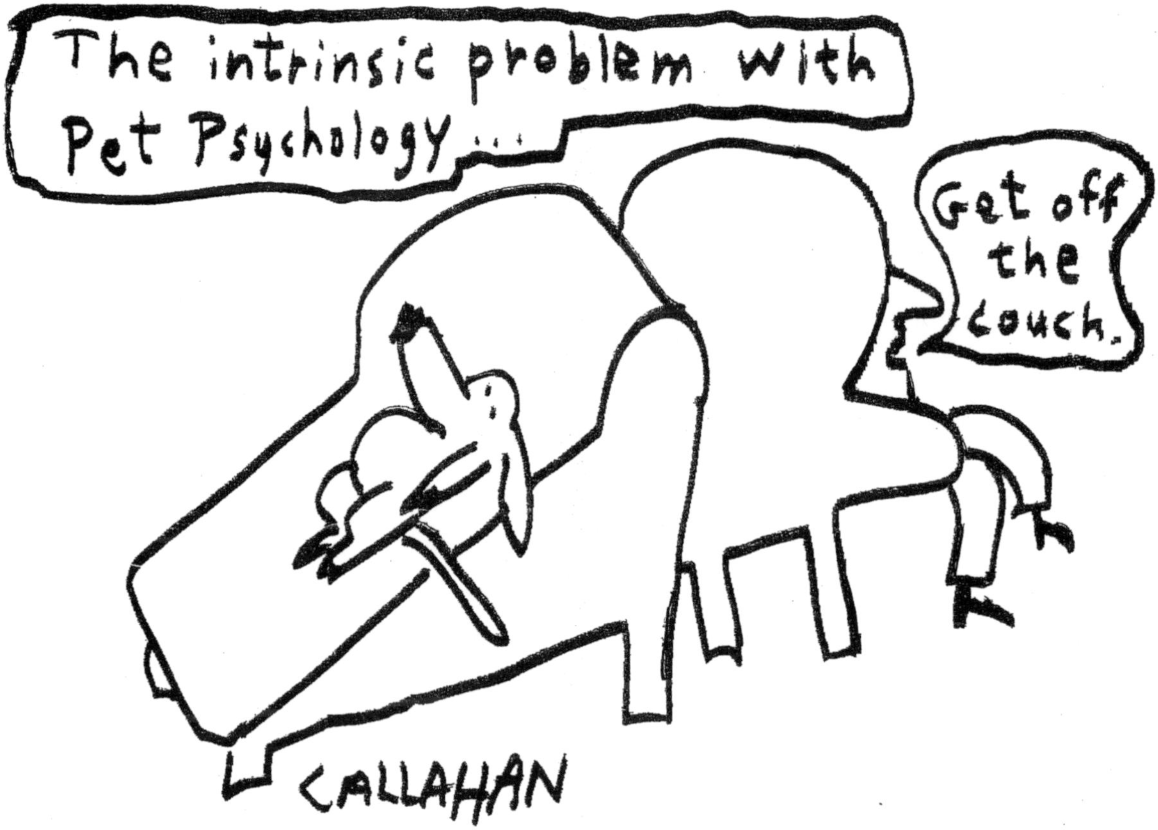
The intrinsic problem with Pet Psychology....
Get off the couch.
CALLAHAN

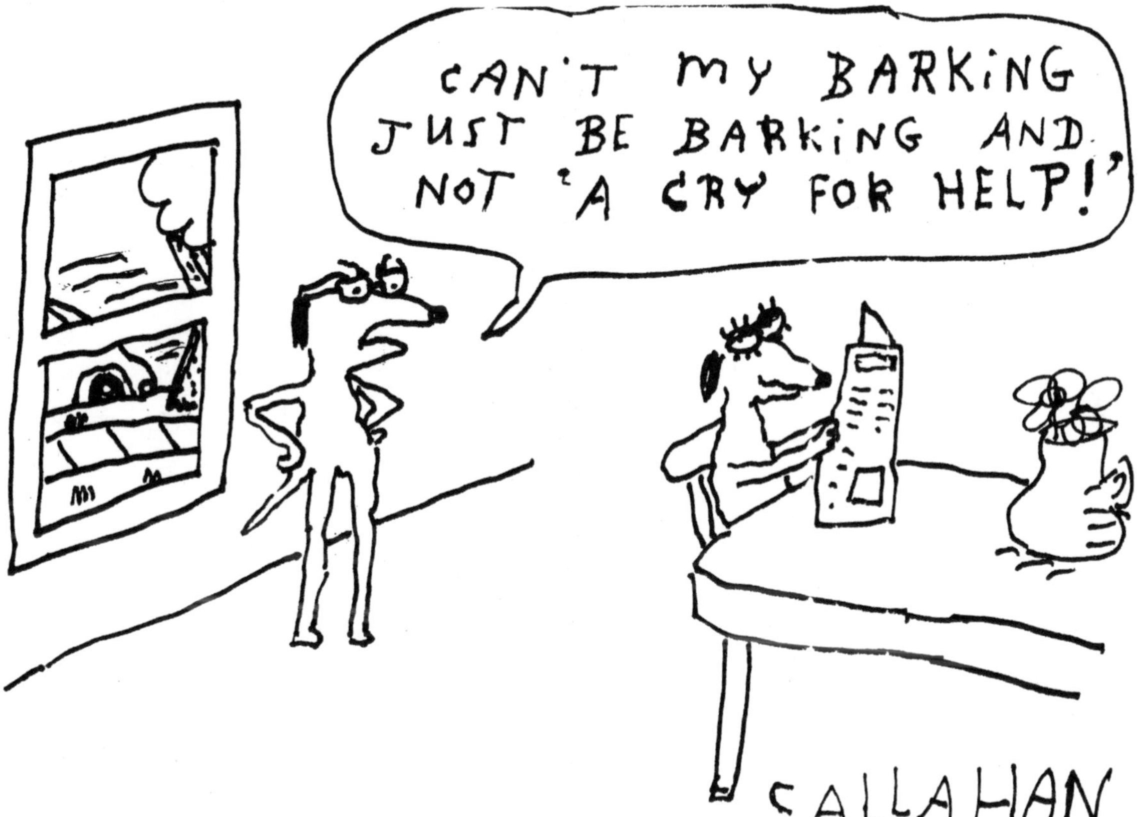
CAN'T MY BARKING JUST BE BARKING AND NOT 'A CRY FOR HELP!'
CALLAHAN

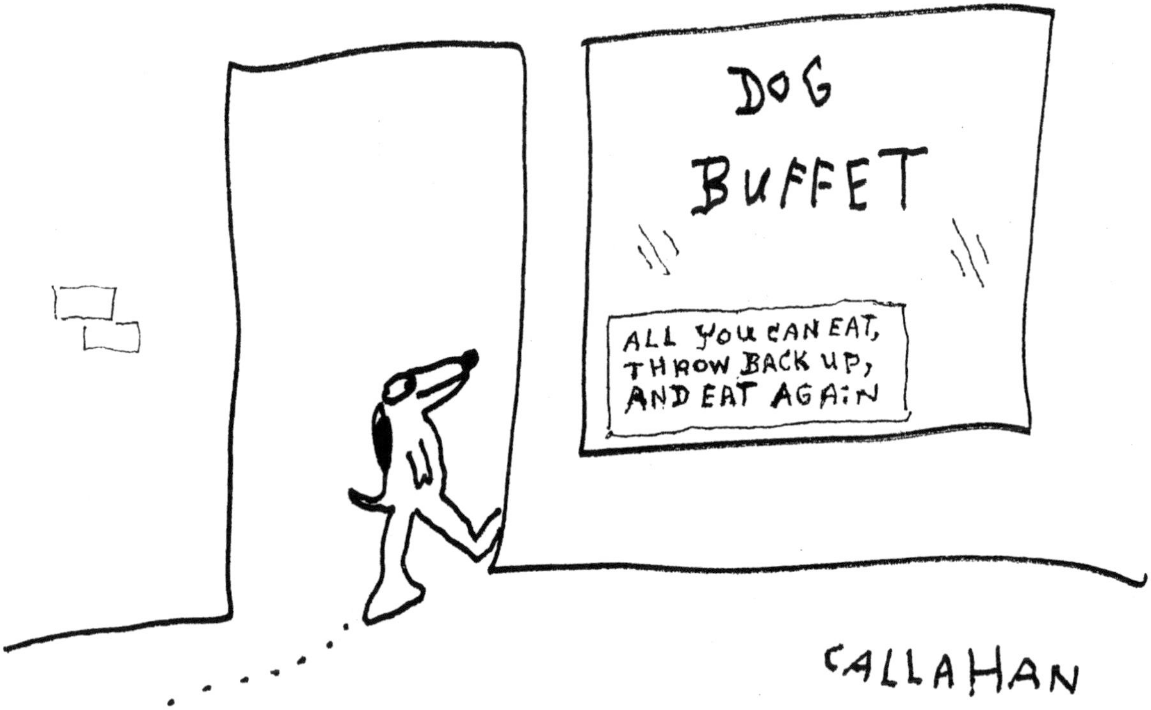
DOG
BUFFET
ALL YOU CAN EAT,
THROW BACK UP,
AND EAT AGAIN
CALLAHAN

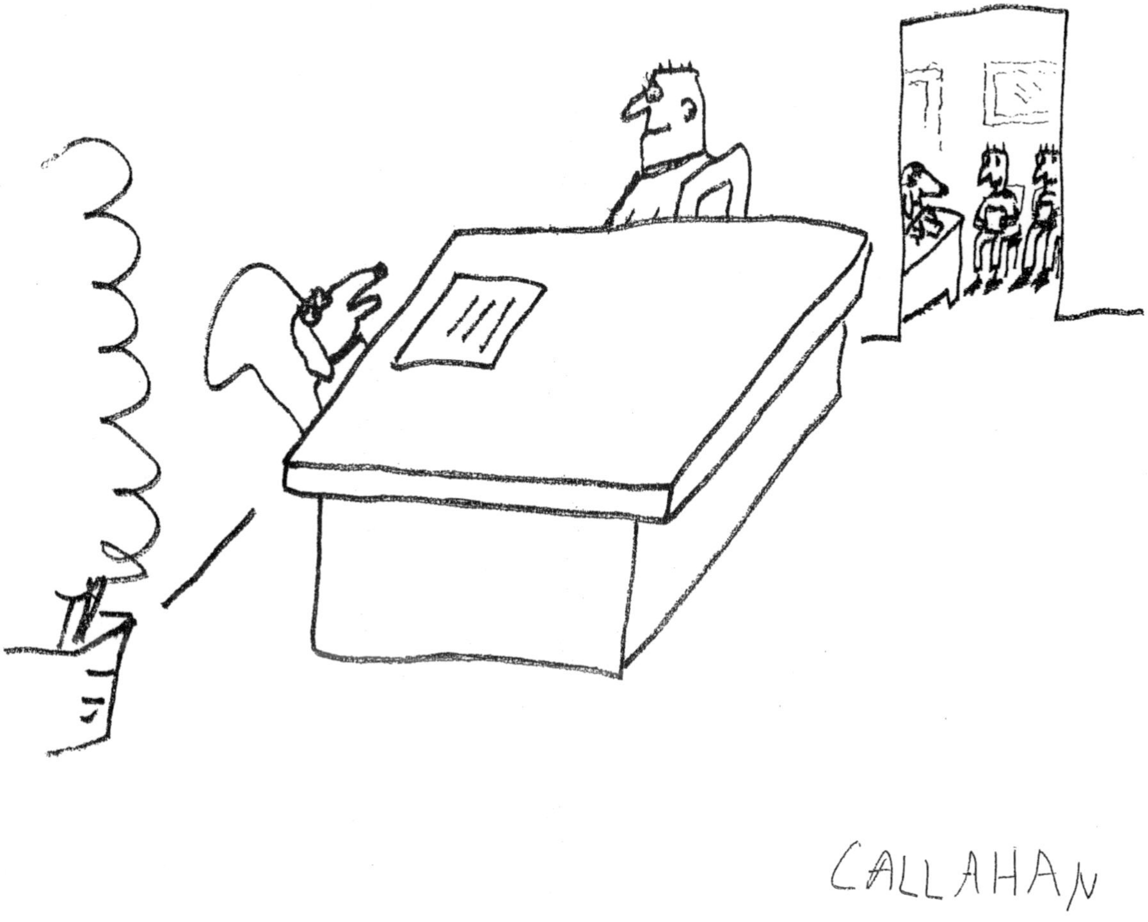
CALLAHAN

"Where do you see yourself walking me?"

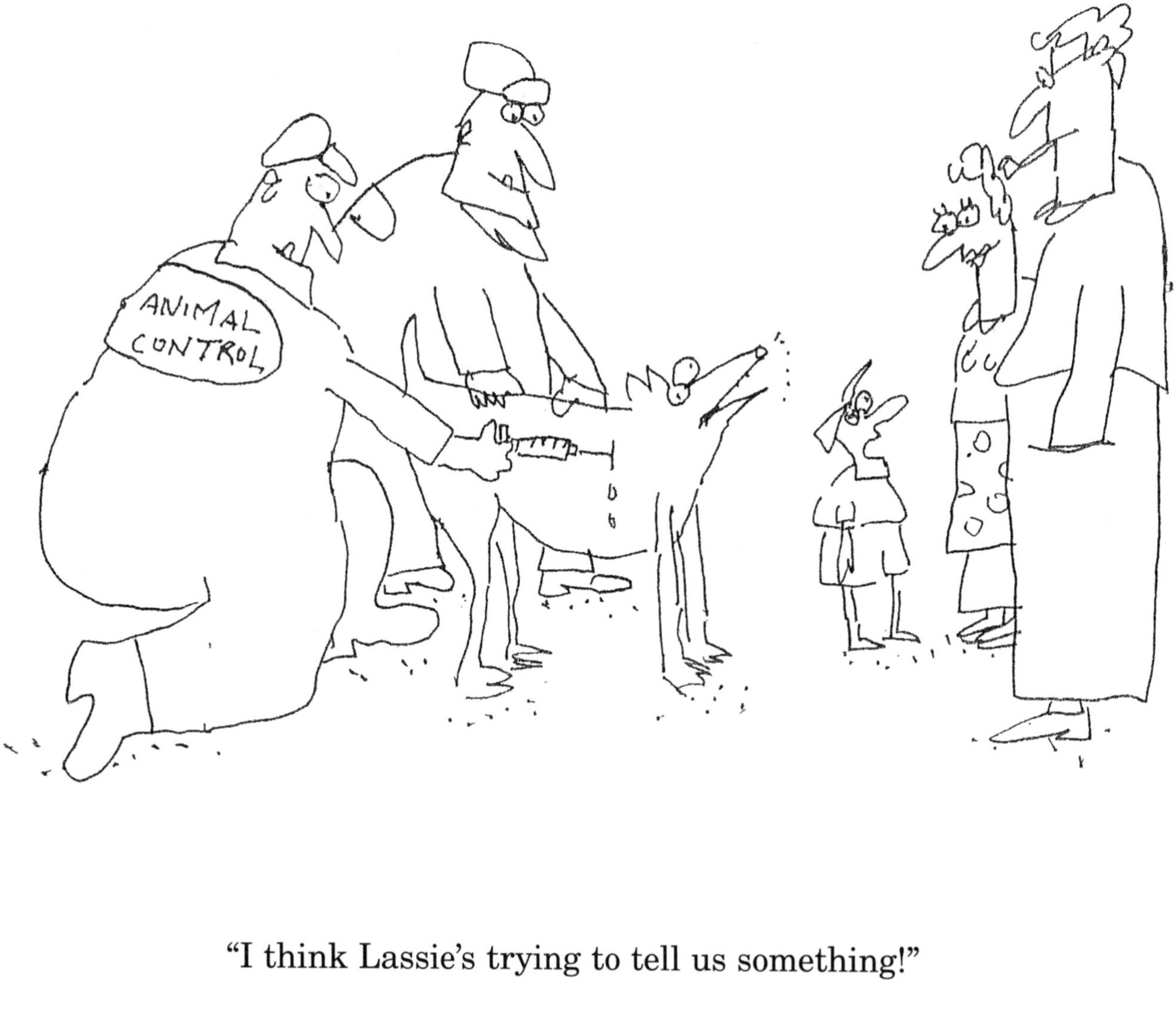
ANIMAL CONTROL

"I think Lassie's trying to tell us something!"

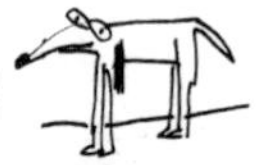

John Callahan is a quadriplegic who was paralyzed in an auto accident in 1972. Since then he has become a famous cartoonist. He has been profiled on *60 Minutes* and NPR's *Fresh Air* with Terry Gross. Callahan lives in Portland, Oregon, where he can be seen buzzing around his neighborhood in his wheelchair. Visit www.callahanonline.com

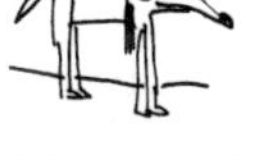